IT ALL COMES OUT IN THE
WASH

IT ALL COMES OUT IN THE
WASH

Sorting Through Priorities
When Your Load Is Out of Balance

JUDI BRADDY

BEACON HILL PRESS
OF KANSAS CITY

Copyright 2006
By Judi Braddy and Beacon Hill Press of Kansas City

ISBN-10: 0-8341-2259-6
ISBN-13: 978-0-8341-2259-8

Printed in the
United States of America

Cover Design: Chad A. Cherry
Interior Design: Sharon Page

Library of Congress Cataloging-in-Publication Data

Braddy, Judi, 1948-
   It all comes out in the wash : sorting through priorities when your load is out of balance / Judi Braddy.
      p. cm.
   Includes bibliographical references.
   ISBN-13: 978-0-8341-2259-8 (pbk.)
   ISBN-10: 0-8341-2259-6 (pbk.)
   1. Time management—Religious aspects—Christianity. 2. Simplicity—Religious aspects—Christianity. 3. Conduct of life. 4. Christian life. I. Title.

   BV4598.5.B73 2006
   248.8'43—dc22

                                                                        2006014741

10 9 8 7 6 5 4 3 2 1

This book is dedicated in loving memory to my mother,
Leona Gladys Witt,
who balanced life more beautifully
than anyone I've ever known.

CONTENTS

PREWASH

It's one of those too-rare Monday mornings. Following a full weekend of ministry-related travel, my family is finally fed, dressed, and out the door. The house is once again quiet. Savoring the silence, I make a fresh pot of coffee, then sit at the kitchen table sipping slowly, staring out the glass patio door as soft shafts of morning sunlight filter in. For once the only pressing appointment I have is with the loads of laundry now happily humming in the washer and dryer down the hall.

Though some might consider it just one more of life's tedious tasks, I've always loved doing laundry. There's just something soothing about the whoosh and whir of the washer and dryer as I go about other tasks. Especially on a cold winter's day, I love the warmth and fragrance it spreads through the house, causing the windows to steam and bringing a snuggled-in sense of well-being in an otherwise inhospitable world; or on a bright, open-window summer day when the clean and crisply folded stacks seem to absorb the sun's warm scent and sparkle.

For me, folding those fragrant fabrics is like aroma therapy, not to mention the routine and repetitive process that requires little thought but produces such an amazing sense of satisfaction. Stepping back and seeing the symmetrical stacks makes me feel that my whole life is once again clean and in order—even if only temporarily.

Face it: from the delicate "unmentionables" to the

brash, colorful cottons, nothing represents the everyday stuff of life like laundry. These are the duds we don to show our style or camouflage our cabooses—stuff that so quickly and easily becomes soiled and wrinkled, needing frequent spot removal if not a deep detergent dunking.

How much more so this is true spiritually speaking.

No doubt the reason we relish those days when things hum so warmly and fuzzily along is that our lives are too often in a very different type of tumble. I know whereof I speak. Not only am I married to a much-in-demand minister who is also a denominational executive, but I'm also busily blessed with my own writing and speaking ministry. Add to that the delightful though often intrusive dynamics of a fairly large family, and it's no surprise that things frequently get a bit out of balance in the Braddy household. And that's not counting the unpredictable parade of unexpected interruptions—and eruptions—that come dressed in every form and fashion.

As a result, I've come to understand that finding time to fall back and regroup is not just special but also crucial to keeping my spiritual, physical, mental, and emotional health and well-being in balance. I believe it's only as we grasp the importance of nurturing this same sense of serenity and order in our spiritual lives that we discover how everything else falls into place under that.

Perhaps you picked up this book because you, too, feel a desperate need to bring balance back into your life but don't know where to start. Before you turn another page, I have good news. You have a friend in the laundry business. His name is Jesus. All you have to do is drop off your dirty duds, ask Him to take care of them, and He'll do the rest. You even get a written guarantee: *"Come now, let us reason together," says the* LORD. *"Though your sins are like scarlet, they shall be as white as snow"* (Isa. 1:18).

The truth for all of us is that no matter how life tumbles us or turns up the heat, no matter how wrinkled or soiled our circumstances, it's God's grace alone that provides the blessed balance we need for everything to truly come out in the wash.

Trust me, my friend. It's nothing short of a wash day miracle.

THE UNBALANCED LOAD

Soak me in your laundry and I'll come out clean,
scrub me and I'll have a snow-white life.
—Ps. 51:7, TM

"Not another one!"

This was the somewhat-less-supportive-than-anticipated response I got from a good friend after telling her about my new book project, one geared toward encouraging women to bring balance back into their lives. Admittedly, it threw me a bit off-balance.

With a significantly softer tone, she continued. "Don't we all know what the problem is by now? We're too busy. Why can't we just figure it out and fix it once and for all?"

IT ALL COMES OUT IN THE WASH

Well, that *is* the question, isn't it?

One that is being continually explored, judging from the number of articles in every major women's magazine on eliminating stress, organizing your time, space, thoughts, and so on.

Obviously my fastidious friend is right. Many articles and books *have* been written outlining the steps for setting boundaries and drawing margins in your life—and, may I add, purchased by the pound, indicating to me an urgent and ongoing need.

Still her comments confirmed something I had already determined. This book would need to take a different twist. Rather than expounding more on the what-to-dos, I decided that exploring the why-we-don'ts might prove more helpful. Now all I needed was a profound theme, one that every woman would relate to.

Of course—laundry.

You see, I have a theory that life is like laundry. If we don't stay on top of it, it piles up quickly and, when neglected too long, can get really stinky. Then what do we do? Instead of taking time to sort things out, we just toss everything into the washer at once to save time. The next thing we know, the machine is overloaded, unbalanced, and dancing out of control. And the items inside? Too soon we discover that either what should be dazzling has come out dingy or, worse, the colors have all run together.

When that happens, it's time to turn off the spin cycle and take a look at how you're handling the home goods.

Of course, we're not talking laundry here but how to

manage our lives and relationships in order to avoid the need for costly future repairs. It's no secret. A machine that's constantly overloaded needs more maintenance and may still eventually break down.

The original adage "It all comes out in the wash" actually means not to worry. Given enough time, everything will eventually come out clean. Nice thought, and still true in some instances. However, today's "wash" has become a lot more complicated. We simply have to realize that the more we stuff in there, the less likely we're going to be pleased with how things turn out.

Unless you live alone on an island—and everyone who saw the movie *Castaway* knows even that has its challenges—life is full of complexities, usually in the form of people, responsibilities, and things. The common solution, in laundry terms, is to sort things out, keep the loads manageable, and maintain the machine. Yet how many times have we resolved to take control of our time or get better organized only to find ourselves a few months later overloaded and overstuffed once again? And maintain the machine? Yeah—like we have time to do that.

So what's a sister caught in the spin cycle to do?

Contrary to popular teaching, the key is not just better time management or optimum organization. Certainly those things can be useful tools in eliminating the clutter from our schedules and spaces. However, based on responses I've received from a vast repertoire of women's retreats, plus my own experience attempting to balance the myriad responsibilities and expectations accompanying 38-plus years of marriage and ministry, I've come to another conclusion: Discipline works long-term only when it's spiritually motivated.

The best motivation for getting our lives in order is to truly understand how much God loves us, what a wonderful plan He has for our lives, and, if given a chance, how He will help us eliminate whatever interferes with it. A certain popular pastor recently wrote a whole book about that—on purpose.

Trouble is, even with the best of motives, it's not going to happen instantly or miraculously. That, my frazzled friend, is where the detergent hits the agitator.

Living in an instant-answer, self-gratifying society, many of us continue seeking a one-time, one-size-fits-all solution. Something we can just plug into our emotional outlet and, *Voila!* From that point on everything balances out and falls into place with minimum effort on our part.

We're also a generation of women who have been told we can do it all. Except we're not even sure what *all* is. Instead, with the breeze of women's liberation blowing in our hair, we continue to take on more and more responsibility, only to end up stressed and depressed when it becomes obvious that trying to do too much inevitably means doing nothing well. *Why, many of us wonder, instead of feeling fulfilled, do I feel as though I can't keep pace with the expectations I've put on myself?*

This brings me to the poignant point my aforementioned friend went on to make, though much more eloquently than I. "The Body of Christ in particular," she lamented, "is still missing the fact that the problems of stress, overload, and balance are really surface-to-root issues. It's much deeper than merely adjusting one's calendar and trying to locate margins, although granted, this would help. Understanding the spiritual root of what our society has evolved into, including the fact that 'the world is too much with us' (a la Wordsworth) is the primary place to start. Without it, I don't think any of us will get accomplished what we're hoping to accomplish, and we certainly won't influence the world for the Lord."

Well said.

Frankly, I'm not convinced that women *want* to do it all. Could it be that much of the added activity we take on boils down to a subconscious search for identity, affirmation, and validity? In our persistent pursuit of being everything for everybody, we just keep adding things on without taking time to prioritize or evaluate what needs to be subtracted. As a result, it's a long, frustrating time before some of us discover where our true God-given gifts and passions really lie.

Whether we put the expectations on ourselves or others put them on us, we don't want to disappoint or shirk our responsibilities, so we simply can't bring ourselves to say no.

Then what happens? We can end up feeling frustrated because we can't control our circumstances, and we feel powerless to pursue our real passions and interests. We may end up resenting our responsibilities and anything, people included, we perceive is keeping us from feeling personally fulfilled.

Life comes in all shapes, sizes, and fabrics. While the permanent press parts of our lives may withstand a little more stress without showing the wear and tear, there are still the parts of our hearts labeled "Handle with care." That's the place where hopes and dreams hover, where our secret longings languish. We can't treat them the same and expect them to hold up.

Some of us have misplaced the care instructions. Many in our society have wandered far from their spiritual moorings. Today's lines of morality have been blurred; nothing is absolute. As a result, many of us are confused about what the roles and responsibilities of women really are. Some bear the emotional scars from unwise choices made based on corrupt counsel. Others live with the consequences of the poor planning of others. We come from broken homes with broken hearts, our foundation for setting solid priorities in crumbles. Is there hope, we wonder, of ever regaining control over our lives and finding joy in our current set of circumstances?

Yes. And therein lies my real reason for writing yet another book on this subject: to share some hopeful insights on life in the laundry room. If nothing else, we need encouragement to know that we're not in there alone.

The truth is that no one lives without stress. If someone claims he or she has successfully eliminated angst from his or her life, check for a pulse. Stress is part of life and may not always be a bad thing. Why? Stress can motivate us to take stock and make improvements. Face it—if our lives worked like a well-oiled machine, there would be no need for improvement.

There would be no need for God.

You see, to be stressed is human, to ask for help, divine. We're human, and as such, we're in need of divine direction. Here's the really good news: once we realize we need His help, God may actually be able to do something wonderful with us.

It has little to do with being skillful or competent. Women have always been amazing in what they can accomplish. Maybe that's part of the problem. We're too good at what we do. My hope is that we can step away from the spin cycle long enough to discover one important thing: the difference between *doing* it all and *becoming* all God wants us to be.

So, ladies, are you ready to do some laundry? Perhaps together we can *Gain* some knowledge that may help us turn the *Tide* and determine the right reasons for making some necessary and important changes—ones custom-made in the right sizes and shapes.

THEY DON'T MAKE A MODEL BIG ENOUGH

You became imitators of us and of the Lord. . . .
You welcomed the message with the joy given by
the Holy Spirit. And so you became a model to all
the believers.
—1 Thess. 1:6-7

The first washing machine my mother
had was a state-of-the-art 1950s electric
model. I remember it well. Like a white
enamel goddess, it sat enthroned on the
enclosed back porch of our tiny Midwestern frame house. Attached to the
round, stainless steel tub was a column
supporting a horizontal metal arm that
encased two round rubber wringers. Following the wash and rinse cycles, my
mother lifted the clothes, piece by piece,
and ran them through the wringers,
squeezing out the excess water before
they went to the "dryer."

In those days a dryer consisted of three lines tautly strung between poles in the backyard, to which Mom attached each item using little wooden gizmos called, logically, clothes pins.

As a child I was fascinated by this process, until the day when, trying to hurry, my mother's fingers got too close to the wringers. In a few frightening seconds, her arm went through right along with the article of clothing she was holding.

It was my first clue that trying to do too much, too fast, can cause things to come back and bite you. Fortunately, Mom managed to hit the emergency release, popping open the wringers before any serious damage was done.

When it comes to being in a hurry and doing too much, I've observed a lot of women in today's world looking for the release lever. I've also observed that, almost without realizing it, we can be our own worst enemy.

Most of us with husbands and children have the same basic desires—to please our husbands, raise families who are happy and healthy, have homes that are sanctuaries of beauty and serenity, and excel in our careers and creative callings. Some might say it's our "wiring."

Every so often, however, those wires get crossed.

One thing that can create a short circuit quicker than sticking your finger in an electric socket is that women, much more so than men, have what seems an almost inborn tendency toward comparison. If not inborn, it's certainly a classic feminine characteristic—one, I've noted in my many travels, that's cultivated in most modern societies. How well I remember on a recent ministry trip to Moscow, watching television in my hotel room and being amazed at what I saw. Though I couldn't understand Russian, it didn't take an interpreter to know what the commercials in particular were implying. The subtle message was "If you want to be a step ahead of everyone else, you need this," meaning whatever product was being promoted. Though we hear this in North America all the time, I was truly surprised to find that message in a faraway society.

In our all-too-familiar North American laundry lingo, it's called "always looking for the new-and-improved model." What happens is that we go along perfectly happy until one day we notice—or someone subtly points out—that somebody else is doing what we thought we were doing but easier, better, and with more style.

Can there be any doubt that the media marketers have plugged into this? Why else would there be a never-ending barrage of magazine ads, daytime television, and talk show commentary picturing what others have, do, wear, want, *ad infinitum*—the majority of whose messages are directed at women?

No wonder it's so easy to lose perspective, causing many of us to determine self-worth in terms of what we have and how we look rather than who we really are. It steers us toward not only overstressing but also overspending, which leads to a completely different type of tension.

Comparison, of course, is not limited to the area of

material possessions. How many times have we caught ourselves coveting someone else's gifts or abilities, wishing, for instance, that we could speak, sing, or play an instrument like that person? This is not to say we shouldn't ask God to reveal and help us develop our own spiritual gifts. Yet how much valuable time and energy do we waste trying to fit into someone else's spiritual slippers?

"All my life I've struggled with the need for success, for tangible signs of approval," wrote Deb Haggerty, a friend I recently met through an online writer's group. "For me that meant being a successful speaker and writer, but roadblocks kept getting in the way of my ideas of success." These came into Deb's life in different forms—first the care of a special-needs stepchild, then moving from place to place because of her husband's career, and finally a bout with breast cancer. "My ideas of success just haven't measured up to my reality," Deb admits. It's hard when things keep interfering not to compare our lives to someone else's and feel we're getting the short end of the straw.

At those times we might do well to heed the words of author Doris Mortman, who said, "Until you make peace with who you are, you'll never be content with what you have." Prov. 14:30 puts a little stronger spin on it: "A heart at peace gives life to the body, but envy rots the bones."

It's a lesson God graciously taught Deb. "This year," she continues, "God helped me see that at this season in my life I am just to 'be.' That to be successful means being the person God intended us to be—whatever the calling at different times along the way." Her main ministry now is to encourage women with breast cancer who want to control their own health care, and their families who want to support them.[1]

Certainly there's no limit to what a determined woman can accomplish. But for our own good, we must pay attention to our inward whispers that remind us of our own physical and emotional limitations, seek God's direction, then take on only the tasks that nurture and support our physical, emotional, and spiritual well-being.

Does that mean God doesn't ask women to take on leadership roles? Of course not. My friend Priscilla comes from a large and distinguished family of ministers. So it was no surprise that she married a minister. For more than 20 years she and her husband served in several successful churches and church-related positions while raising two children. They portrayed the perfect pastoral family—until the day Priscilla's husband informed her that he no longer loved her. Sick with shock, she eventually discovered there had been more than one carefully hidden incidence of marital unfaithfulness over the years.

After her husband left, Priscilla wisely spent a few years putting the pieces of her life back together. Though reeling with personal rejection, she had a number of things going for her. A woman of spiritual strength with strong family support, she was also blessed with many gifts and talents. And she wasn't afraid to work. For years as a pastor's wife, she had planned and implemented major church events. Eventually, drawing on her experience in hospitality and culinary arts, she created a successful catering business. Geared toward churches, this provided her ministry while also paying the bills. Most important, however, it was something she loved, filling the empty spaces in her life with personal joy and satisfaction.

Imagine Priscilla's greater delight when her ministry experience, planning expertise, and organizational skills attracted the attention of her denomination's leadership, leading to an appointment as district women's ministries director. This is a high-level position serving with peers of both genders, one she has filled capably and with much joy for the last 10 years.

Though the circumstance leading up to this was one that Priscilla would never have chosen, and this was a role she might not have otherwise sought or anticipated, it's obvious that God not only saw her need but also knew her qualifications long before she did.

Along with His confidence in her capabilities, God threw in an added perk: He replaced her mourning with joy. Joy, in case you've forgotten, is not just another brand of dishwashing detergent. Prov. 10:28 tells us, "The prospect of the righteous is joy, but the hopes of the wicked come to nothing." Joy is something every believer should expect to experience.

Unfortunately, however, our joy sometimes gets submerged in the suds of serving others.

You see, one other potential downside of a woman's nurturing nature is that it often causes us to take on the role of caregivers for everyone else. That's not necessarily a bad thing. After all, serving is biblical, right? Yes, unless we somehow become convinced that everyone's happiness and well-being depends entirely on us. It's then our lives may become so entwined with the lives of others that we forget not only who we are as gifted individuals but also what our spiritual priorities should be.

Martha is a great example. No, not Martha Stewart, though she might certainly be the modern-day equivalent. I'm talking about the Martha spoken of in Luke 10:38-41, the hostess with the mostest. Who better to become the biblical poster child for doing all the right things for all the wrong reasons?

In case you need a review, here's the story. Martha lived with her sister, Mary, and brother, Lazarus, in a town near Jerusalem called Bethany. They were, according to correlating passages of Scripture, dear friends of Jesus who often opened their home to Him as a respite. In this particular passage, upon Martha's hearing that Jesus and His disciples were on their way, her nurturing nature kicked into overdrive. Her cooking and cleaning frenzy was evidently such that scripture describes her as being "distracted by all the preparations that had to be made" (v. 40). What really got her into trouble, though, was that in her state of self-induced delirium she ended up angry and resentful with her sister, Mary, for not helping. Interesting, isn't it, how when we're being driven to distraction we want to stop and pick up passengers? Mary, it seems, had chosen instead to "[sit] at the Lord's feet listening to what he said" (v. 39).

Now I ask you. Was Martha wrong for wanting things well prepared for her friends, or, for that matter, wanting someone to help her? No, it's just that somewhere before supper Martha stepped over the legal stress limit. Jesus pinpointed the real problem in verses 41-42 when He said (I imagine with a smile and a sigh), "Martha, Martha . . . you are worried and upset about many things, but only one thing is needed. Mary has chosen what is better."

Can't you just see Martha's lower lip begin to quiver?

Could it be that this wasn't the only time Martha worried about too many things—or, like some of us with time-challenged temperaments, put too many things off to the last minute, then tried to impose her type-A tyranny on others in the household. Perhaps it wasn't the first time, either, that her worries placed her in jeopardy of missing what was really most important: being with Jesus and listening to what He had to say.

You see, my frenzied feminine friend, in spite of our best intentions, it's our very nature that sometimes has us up to the elbow in the wringer of life. Truth is, we don't always do ourselves or others a favor by taking on their needs and stresses. Sometimes it can even backfire and produce the opposite of what we intended. Instead of an environment of calm, we create an atmosphere of chaotic codependency. Instead of being encouragers, we become enablers. Not only does this inevitably produce more work and frustration for us, but it can even rob others of needed life skills, those gained only by taking up their own share of the responsibility. It can also rob others of time to savor the Savior in their own way and time.

No wonder we wake up one day to discover that somewhere in the putting-others-first process we've become slaves to doing and giving to the point that we've lost the joy of serving—not to mention, as in Martha's case, the art of listening.

My friend Joanna Weaver has written a wonderful in-depth book on this scriptural passage entitled *Having a Mary Heart in a Martha World*. I highly recommend it. Listen to her personalization of Jesus' words to Martha: "He's calling us to the Great Exchange—the one where we can never lose. As we trade the 'many things' that make us anxious, he gives us the 'one thing' that calms our hearts. Himself."[2]

There are so many things in our feminine nature that can cause us to take on too much. Face it—some of us just plain like to be busy. That's not necessarily a problem unless somehow we've started equating activity with productivity when often it's just the opposite. Or we worry that if we're not doing something all the time, others may regard us as lazy. Soon we have so many plates spinning that they, and we, are flying off in every direction, sometimes even failing to finish one project before dashing on to the next.

Then there's the pride issue. Things must be done a particular way (usually ours), so we drive ourselves and everyone else crazy with our perfectionism. Perhaps we've cultivated a reputation for creativity or cleverness that we can't bear losing. Some of us are just plain control freaks. We can't let down or let go for fear that things will not get done properly—then others will think we're incompetent, disorganized, or incapable.

I wonder. Could it be that some of us stay busy in order to avoid other real but less-relished responsibilities? Or could it be that it's our way of staying one step ahead of some unresolved regret, that we fear the mask covering our see-through insecurity might fall off, revealing the real person behind the persona? Perhaps what we do has become so much a part of who we are that we're terrified of letting go for fear that we won't recognize ourselves apart from it.

What about those of us driven by our own inner critic, one that may even mimic the toxic tones of some negative voice from our past telling us "No matter how hard you try, it will never be good enough."

These points touch on issues woven so deeply into the fabric of our inherited character that we often don't even realize it. Those cases may require a special spot-removing treatment, something author Jan Coleman addresses personally in her book *The Woman Behind the Mask*. "Like me," she writes, "you may have been piling on the masks for years, and you've played so many roles you're not sure which one is you. Becoming an authentic woman means . . . going beneath the persona to find the real woman, discover your original voice and tempo . . . find the parts of your personality you despised and suppressed. We have to be open emotionally and spiritually for the Lord to define who we are."[3]

The bottom line is this: Whatever has our agitators on overdrive, it's probably because we're expecting more of ourselves than even God does. No wonder that before we know it, some of us have taken on loads so large that (no offense to the Prov. 31 woman) they don't make a model big enough to handle it.

By the way, according to my pastor-husband, most biblical scholars agree that the woman described in Prov. 31:10-31 is a composite character. While all the things she is depicted as doing are qualities to be admired and emulated, the writer never intended to convey that these are things every woman should be doing all day, every day. If you are, it's more likely that instead of *blessed*, your family will rise up and call you *stressed*.

Laundry lovers, it's time for an extreme think-over. What exactly is it that God requires of us? According to 1 Cor. 4:1-2, there's only one thing: "So then, men ought to regard us as servants of Christ and as those entrusted with the secret things of God. Now it is required that those who have been given a trust must prove faithful."

That's it? That's all God asks of us—to be faithful?

Right.

"But—but—don't you understand?" we stammer. "That's all I'm trying to do—be faithful!"

Yes, but to whom? Others? Yourself? God? Perhaps the more important question is "In what order?"

It's admirable, even scriptural, that we pursue everything with excellence. "Whatever you do," states Col. 3:23-24, "work at it with all your heart." Now here's the clincher: "as working for the Lord, not for men, since you know that you will receive an inheritance from the Lord as a reward. It is the Lord Christ you are serving."

Our why-we-don't dilemma seems to come in the form of distinguishing for whom we're working and for what ultimate reward.

How much simpler, or at least less confusing, life would be if we could get our spiritual priorities straight, then allow everything else to fall into place under that, to understand that being a Christian requires not so much doing great (or many) things as it requires taking time to do the ordinary, everyday things greatly.

Still thinking that may require a wash day miracle? I have good news. God is continually in the cleanup business, and He knows the particular product to use for every type of fabric.

Who, after all, could be more intimately familiar with the fabric of our lives than He who "created [our] inmost being" and "knit [us] together in [our] mother's womb"? (Ps. 139:13) The way we are is no surprise to God. He's intimately acquainted with our many flaws and frustrations. He knows us better than we know ourselves and—here's the big breakthrough—loves us anyway. That doesn't mean, however, that there isn't room for improvement. It was Leighton Ford who said, "God loves us the way we are, but He loves us too much to leave us that way."

Somehow in all the busyness of our lives, God wants to weave His will and way in us. He alone knows the great potential in the pattern He has planned for our lives. That's the new-and-improved model we need to be seeking.

THE FABRIC
OF OUR LIVES

You know exactly how I was made, bit by bit, how
I was sculpted from nothing into something.
—Ps. 139:15, TM

For me there's no such thing as a quick trip to the fabric store. No matter what I dash in for, the minute my eyes alight on all the vivid tints and textures, I'm captivated. Soon I'm dreamily wandering the aisles, unable to keep my fingers from caressing the myriad materials. The possibilities seem endless and exciting. As an avid seamstress, I view purchasing a pattern and piece of fabric like already having a new outfit. The reality is that until the pattern is cut out and the parts sewn together, any fabric, no matter how beautiful, is just a piece of cloth with potential.

Like us.

Symbolically speaking, our lives are comprised of many different threads, all being woven, then pieced together to form a particular pattern. Imagine, for instance, the makings of a beautiful quilt.

My friend Alice Alford, a quilter extraordinaire, claims that each quilt she crafts tells a story. Each takes many months, sometimes even years, to complete. See the similarities? Likewise, our life stories are being pieced together one stitch at a time. Then, of course, there are the crazy quilts, made up of all the leftover bits and pieces, but we won't go there except to say that with the Master Quilter's creative touch, even they can be turned into something fun and colorful.

It's a good thing, too, because the truth is that on many days most of us have a hard time just getting the wrinkles out of the fabric of our lives—not to mention the times we end up feeling frayed around the edges or, worse, coming unraveled. It's those days we may spend a lot of time and energy running around, struggling just to regain control when perhaps what we really need is to stop and regain composure. Consider a lesson from my young friend Trevor.

At a large gathering of Trevor's family, the adults— busy visiting and cooking—left the youngsters to devise their own entertainment. Predictably, this soon escalated into a mad kid-chase through the house. Just as things reached the point of requiring adult intervention, Trevor suddenly raced in. "I'm outta control!" he announced. "I'm giving myself a time out!" and plopped down in the middle of the floor to do just that.

Ah, for Trevor's wisdom. But we're responsible adults, right? We know when we're racing around haphazardly and need to slow down.

Right.

I suppose it's safe to assume that anyone who has been a believer in Christ for any length of time has been impressed more than once with the importance of personal daily devotions. Some call it "quiet time"—a time set aside for Bible reading and prayer, perhaps including some type of supplemental study guide or additional inspirational reading.

Judging from my own experience, it's also pretty safe to assume that many of us don't manage to do it on any consistent basis. Not that we don't want to, mind you, or that we don't understand the importance. It's just that too often, as we've all heard, "Life is what happens while we're making other plans."

Therein, of course, lies the danger.

We've already discussed how easily our nature can get us in trouble. Again, sometimes we're our own worst enemies when it comes to getting completely off track. Never mind outside distractions. Some of us have such a hard time staying focused that we interrupt ourselves. All it takes is one early-morning phone call, an interesting newspaper article, or a television talk show, and zoom! We've digressed and derailed from our ever-so-pious plans.

Then there are the high-tech interruptions. Faster than

a speeding e-mail, never have so many been interrupted so quickly by so few. I finally promised the Lord I wouldn't even open my e-mails in the morning until I had opened His Word. Which makes me think—wouldn't it be great if someone invented a Bible from which, every time you walked by, a voice like the one Charlton Heston heard in *The Ten Commandments* rumbled, "You've got mail!" That would surely get our attention.

No doubt those with children, jobs, or both have an even more difficult time. First there's the mad rush out the door in the mornings, everyone dashing off in different directions. Then in the evenings there's dinner to fix, homework to do, and chores to catch up on, not to mention the many extracurricular activities we wield and wedge in between. Let's be honest. Unless you're the superdisciplined type who can get up at the crack of dawn before the rest of your hurried household, or you have a brain that doesn't turn to mush by about 9 P.M., the probability of getting much in the way of quiet time is pretty low. I'm ashamed to admit that when my three boys were small, not only did I not eat a hot meal for about eight years, but my daily devotions often went on the back burner as well.

It's always easier, of course, to blame our lack of discipline on someone else. One of the classic cartoons in my illustrations file shows a man and wife sitting on the couch as he peruses his much-marked appointment calendar. The caption, indicating his wife's commentary, reads, "God loves you, and everyone else has a wonderful plan for your life."

It's meant to be a humorous take-off on the first of the Four Spiritual Laws known so well in Evangelical circles: "God loves you and has a wonderful plan for your life." Even if you're not familiar with the saying, the truth behind the humor is obvious. It's amazing how quickly and easily, if we aren't intentional, interruptions—self-made or otherwise—can keep us from that all-important personal time with God. It's especially difficult, and easier to defend, when these come in the shape of things we love and feel obliged to tend, like people or spiritual responsibilities. Yet aren't these the very things we most often need divine direction in dealing with?

In case you have any doubt about the importance of spending time each day renewing your faith and focus, allow me a short stint on the old soapbox.

First of all, God *does* have a wonderful plan for your life, but, just like my experience in the fabric store, it's so easy for us to be lured away by the world's kaleidoscope of colors. Certainly there's much in the world to be enjoyed and admired, but there's also a lot of devil-inspired danger. From Genesis on, it's pretty apparent why we shouldn't be walking around out there alone.

Besides, we need detailed washing instructions. How can our day possibly be cut according to God's pattern if we don't take time to read the directions? The psalmist puts it in spot-removing rhetoric: "How can a young [woman] keep [her] way pure?" then answers: "By living according to your word" (Ps. 119:9). Quite simply, we can't possibly know God's will unless we know God's Word.

Along with giving divine direction, the ways God's Word enriches and enables us are myriad. To get an idea, read the entirety of Ps. 119. His Word is a light to our path, keeps us from sinning, strengthens, preserves, and instructs, to name a very few. Young Pastor Timothy echoes it back from the New Testament: "All scripture is God-breathed and is useful for teaching, rebuking, correcting and training in righteousness, so that the man [or woman] of God may be thoroughly equipped for every good work" (2 Tim. 3:16-17). Thoroughly equipped—I like that. After all, doesn't every empowered woman need her own toolbox?

We also need protection. Certainly there are many outside influences that come into our lives and attempt to offer spiritual instruction. But take heed. Any advice received, no matter how trustworthy it appears, must always line up with God's Word. That means you have to know what it says or where to research any confusing or questionable counsel—not just one isolated verse either, but the entire chapter for proper context. Think of it like never getting onto a motorcycle without a helmet. Knowing God's Word has kept more than one careening Christian from crashing and receiving severe head or heart injuries.

Here's another amazing thing. I can't tell you how many times the scripturally inspired reading from my morning devotions has found personal application later in my day. Wow! God prepares me for my day by weaving His Word into it. Matt. 6:8 puts it this way: "Your Father knows what you need before you ask him."

Then if God already knows what we need, you may be thinking, *what's the point of taking time to pray every day?*

I'm glad you asked.

First and foremost, prayer is a scriptural commandment. As such, Jesus, who is our spiritual example, not only modeled it for us personally but left us a wonderful formula to follow. It's no coincidence that His sample supplication, commonly known as The Lord's Prayer, is recorded in Matt. 6:9 immediately following the scripture just quoted. Now I ask you, if Jesus felt the need to pray regularly and often, how much more do you suppose we need it?

Remember, too, that prayer is much more than just asking for things. According to this scriptural schematic, prayer contains three basic components: Praise, petitions for personal needs, and petitions for others.

Ps. 100:4 instructs us, "Enter his gates with thanksgiving and his courts with praise; give thanks to him and praise his name." Want immediate access to God? Begin your prayers with praise, and you'll be ushered right through His gates and into His presence.

As for our own needs and those of others, though God is already intimately acquainted with them, He still wants us to ask. Why? Like any good parent, God desires to grant His children's requests. However, if He simply answered them indiscriminately, how would that build our faith? We would probably end up taking more for granted than we already do.

Then there are the times when, for reasons we may

not be spiritually mature enough to understand, God has to say no. When that happens, according to Phil. 4:6-7, He promises us peace in His greater, though often unseen, purpose—if we'll only talk to Him.

Quite simply, it's as if through His Word and prayer we take hold of God's hand. And He never lets go. He's like the friend spoken of in Prov. 18:24 "who sticks closer than a brother"—a *big* brother. Understanding this enables us to pray with assurance, *Lord, nothing is going to happen today that you and I can't handle together.* Perhaps even more in keeping with our theme is the quote painted on a wooden heart hanging from a corkboard near my desk: "A day hemmed in prayer seldom unravels."

This brings me to the most important reason for making time to meet with God—one which, in our rush to merely fulfill our devotional duty, we often miss. Both through His word and in prayer, God wants to talk to us, too.

Remember a verse quoted in the last chapter, 1 Cor. 4:1—"Men ought to regard us as servants of Christ and as those entrusted with the secret things of God." Imagine for a moment: Creator God, the Maker of the universe, desires to whisper in our ears His own selected secrets. If we'll take the time to learn and listen, we'll come forth from our prayer closets wearing His wisdom, accessorized by our own specially fitted garments of grace. In textile terms, spending time with Him causes His Word, will, and ways to be woven into the very fabric of our lives, producing a richness and luster that others can't help but notice.

The real test of any garment is how well it will wash and wear. This depends entirely on what it's made of. Even those who prefer to shop rather than sew quickly learn there's a big difference in fabric, and the ones that result in a good-quality garment usually require a greater investment. How much are we willing to invest to ensure that our spiritual garments will be wash-and-wear worthy?

Too many times we come before the Lord out of duty or fear, hoping that the more we do, the more He'll do for us. Too often we never see that our time spent with Him is what the apostle Paul describes as our "reasonable service," a way of showing gratitude for what He's already done for us.

One of my favorite life verses is Rom. 5:8—"God demonstrates his own love for us in this: While we were still sinners, Christ died for us." Imagine—long before we even acknowledged Him, God saw a potential in us that we didn't even recognize in ourselves. This resulted in His sending His only Son to bridge the gap sin created, providing a way for us back to himself. Why, do you suppose, knowing the great sacrifice Christ made, do we seem to spend the majority of our days running in the opposite direction? No investment of our time is anything compared to the investment that God, through Christ, has made in us.

My husband was privileged to be one of only a few ministers in our area invited to a private previewing of Mel Gibson's marvelous film *The Passion of the Christ*. The radical but realistic portrayal of what Christ endured before and during His crucifixion moved him to the core. "I'll never take communion the same way again," he stated solemnly when trying to describe it. Those who saw it will surely understand.

The key to enriching the fabric of our lives is an intentional weaving-together of ourselves with the One who can help us set our priorities according to His pattern, not our own. "Take my yoke upon you," Jesus calls to us, "and learn from me" (Matt. 11:29).

"Wait a minute," you say. "Yokes sound heavy. I thought we were talking about lightening up here, not taking on more."

Read Matt. 11:28-30. Jesus says His yoke is easy and His burden is light (v. 30). That's because He never asks us to take on more than we're able to handle. When that happens, it's usually because we've slipped the yoke and ventured back out on our own. Being yoked together with Him ensures that we stay on the path with Him. It also means that, should the Lord ask us to temporarily bear a heavier burden, He's right there beside us to share it.

Oh, how this helps with the tough decisions we encounter in life, often eliminating other options and a lot of unnecessary frustration! As a reminder of this, I have a poster hanging in my sewing room drawn by artist Mary Englebreit. It shows a young traveler who has come to a crossroads in the woods. Above him are two signs pointing in opposite directions. The one he has chosen reads, "Your Life," and the other, "No Longer an Option." The poster states simply, "Don't Look Back."

Dear sister in the suds, undoubtedly there will be those days when we fall exhausted into bed at night, only to realize we haven't even taken time that day to glance in God's direction. That's when it will help to remember that, unlike us, God isn't on any time schedule. Any hour of the day or night that we turn our thoughts toward Him, He's there, looking lovingly back.

Ps. 139 is a beautiful reminder of how well God knows our comings and goings, our inner weavings. To put it plainly, He knows how we're all going to make it through the wash. Much of that depends on our staying with the pattern He gives us. To do so, we need His daily direction. Take heart. In the process we'll be storing up the materials needed to reinforce us on the days when our frail fabric is being stretched thin.

WHAT HAPPENED TO THE OTHER SOCK?

In his heart a man plans his course, but the LORD determines his steps.
—Prov. 16:9

Inevitably it happens. Just when we think we have the loads in our lives balanced and everything under control, something comes up missing—just like that pesky sock that mysteriously ends up being eaten by the dryer. I mean, what other explanation could there possibly be? It was there when you put the clothes in, right? Now it's gone.

How often it seems that the same thing happens to the plans we make. In only a matter of moments, even life's best-drawn blueprint not only fades drastically but can disintegrate altogether in the heat of extenuating circumstances.

Believe me—I know.

Thirty-eight years ago with eyes full of stardust and a heart full of idealistic (albeit unrealistic) fervor, I married a minister. I thought I knew what the sacrifices of ministry were all about. After all, I had spent one whole year in Bible college and been to a lot of missionary services.

Sure enough, the confirmation came quickly! Within six months of marriage, my husband accepted a position as a youth pastor at a fairly large church near San Diego, and we were called upon to leave family and friends in the Midwest. It was the farthest I had ever been from home on a permanent basis, and I cried through two states. It was definitely tough!

Then we hit California, and I saw the palm trees and beaches. *Could it be that we made a wrong turn near Albuquerque*, I wondered, *and ended up in heaven?*

The church provided us with a three-bedroom home and a salary that allowed us to purchase new furniture and trade our old car for a brand-new '68 Firebird. Let me tell you, Honey—for the next two and a half years we suffered for Jesus! We suffered through beach parties, coffee house ministry, and trips to Disneyland. At age 19 I was only two years older than many of the girls in the youth group, so I got to spend a lot of time doing some, like, really intense relating. In all seriousness, it was an amazing experience.

Needless to say, I settled quickly and sassily into my new surroundings.

Then one deceptively quiet, balmy afternoon a phone call came that would soon relegate all that to a lovely memory. You see, my husband had a sordid past that I had tried to forget. He and his college roommate had spent two summers in a small fishing village in Alaska working at a fish processing plant to make money for college. His roommate's mom was the missionary at the one and only church where the guys had also served as ministry interns. Following graduation, Jim's roommate and his new bride had gone back to pastor this remote mission station. Now, two and a half years later, they were leaving to thaw out and were looking for a replacement pastor.

Thus the phone call.

Before I knew what had happened, my husband, spurred by a sharp nudge of nostalgia, accepted. My reaction? I crumpled onto the couch in tears. Not because I was angry or didn't agree with his decision, but because suddenly our picture-perfect life had some frost around the edges. Even so, in my heart I knew this was exactly what God wanted us to do.

Faster than you can say "Chichagof Island," we sold everything we had accumulated and were there, freshly deposited by an old Grumman "goose" seaplane at the Pelican, Alaska, Metropolitan Airport. This "airport" consisted of a floating platform connected to the shore by a long boardwalk supported by piers. Fact is, when I looked closely I realized that *everything* in town was connected to the shore by a long boardwalk supported by piers. The buildings resembled the replicas I had seen of old Western storefront buildings back in Kansas, and just barely visible on the top of one hill was the cross of the little white church—my home for the next year or more. *Dear Lord*, I remember thinking, *I'm living in Cowtown!*

Pelican, Alaska, population 90, located on an island in the southeast panhandle of the state, accessible only by boat or plane—it was a pretty big change from San Diego, to say the least. Perhaps it was only the wind blowing off the surrounding snow-capped mountains, but I was sure I heard a voice that day saying, "Hold on, Honey—this is just the beginning!"

And it was.

Now, 38 years, 26 moves, three children, and five grandchildren later, why do I tell you this? So you'll know that I've learned a little bit over the years about changing circumstances and the emotions that accompany them. But it's also to assure you that what I considered at the time to be a major interruption in my picture-perfect life ended up being perhaps the most important year of our marriage and ministry.

More experiences were packed into those few months than I have space here to write about. That would require another book, one I might tackle someday, titled *Everything I Needed to Know About Life I Learned in Pelican, Alaska*. Suffice it to say, in a town that size with only six other professing Christians, Jim and I were about all we had. Because of that, we learned to depend totally on the Lord and each other. When we had problems, we had no choice but to stay and work them out. There was literally no place else to go—at least no easy way to get there.

Our biggest challenge that year was joyfully discovering I was pregnant with our first child, only to suffer the sadness of a miscarriage a few weeks later. By the time we left a year later, we felt we had pretty much run the gamut of experience and emotion. We also came away knowing that if we could survive that year, we could probably survive anything else life might dish out. Thirty-plus years later, it turns out we were right.

We've all heard the saying "The best-laid plans of mice and men often go astray." When I hear it, I get this mental picture of a group of scientists in a room full of cages with tiny, gray creatures navigating mazes, sniffing out the cheese waiting at the other end.

Do you ever wonder if God sees us that way? Little humans scurrying here, there, and everywhere, following first one path and then another in an attempt to reach some elusive goal. We have the best intentions. After all, we're on a mission for the heavenly cheese, so to speak.

The amazing truth is that God cares for both mice and men (and women). Each is His creation, but we're the ones made in His image, with eternity woven into the fabric of our hearts. That's why it's so important to Him that we not get too far off track. No wonder He sometimes has to tap us on the shoulder and say, "Excuse Me—how about taking a little time out?"

I've come to believe that the majority of things we consider interruptions in our lives are actually God's attempt to bring—OK, in some cases, *yank*—us back onto the right path. At the very least, He wants us to stop long enough to get our bearings and examine our priorities. All undoubtedly serve the purpose of teaching us compassion and patience.

This was part of the lesson learned by my online author friend Deb Haggerty. One thing Deb considered at that time to be a roadblock to her writing and speaking ministry was the care of her then-six-year-old stepson, James, a child with special needs. Two years ago, James was tragically killed in an automobile accident. "How thankful I was then," says Deb, "for those years with James!" It was also during this time, as hundreds of cards and letters poured in, that God let Deb know how many people's hearts she had touched through her life and ministry.

What we have to take into consideration is that God, being—well—God, sees things from a different perspective than we do. His plan involves the whole world. Isn't it amazing to think that we're all part of His greater design, yet He still takes time to care what happens in each individual life? Somehow I find great comfort in the fact that while we're on earth feverishly working out our paltry plans, God is in heaven working out *the* plan. You see, He really does want us to find the cheese.

"But why is it," you may ask, "that some interruptions are so much more painful than others?"

Remember growing pains? These were the phantom joint aches that sometimes kept us awake as children when our bodies took a sudden growing spurt. Could it be that we simply can't grow spiritually either, without being stretched? Obviously that's going to involve some pain. We don't like it, nor do we always understand it, but it's going to happen. "Pain is inevitable," says well-known author and speaker Barbara Johnson, "but misery is optional."

Sometimes these are opportunities God allows so we can experience a new season of personal growth in our lives. After a devastating divorce, my friend Jan admits that she turned into her single season with dread, "as if I were a captive Jew," she writes in her book *The Woman Behind the Mask*, "bound hand and foot by the Babylonians, carried kicking and screaming into exile." It was during this season, however, that she began to discover her talents and gifts and that she could use them in ministry. "Imagine my surprise," Jan reflects now, "to find myself content after a few years of going solo. The season turned out to be more enjoyable than I imagined—and to think I almost turned it down."[1]

So what keeps us not just holding on through these inevitable, sometimes painful, changes, but actually enjoying the ride? It comes down to two things: our choice of attitude and our choice of action.

A year after the World Trade Centers in New York City were attacked, *Woman's Day* magazine ran an article written by Marnell Jameson entitled "Bouncing Back," which focused on those with the ability to recover when life throws a curve.[2] The highlights of the article covered things such as reining in emotions—that is, not feeling sorry for yourself or grieving too long, determining to make something good come out of even the worst situations, having a flexible style of thinking so as to see situations more accurately, reaching out for help, even finding humor in the pain. The significant sidebar, however, quoted Andrew Shatte of the University of Pennsylvania and said this: "The more you are connected with things bigger than yourself the more resilient you will be."

There's nothing bigger in our lives than God. My experience has been that the best way to keep our attitudes and actions in check is to keep our eyes on Him. In this way we focus not on what changes in our lives but on what remains constant.

One of my favorite life verses is found in the first chapter of James: "Every good and perfect gift is from above, coming down from the Father of the heavenly lights, who does not change like shifting shadows" (v. 17). I especially love the more poetic wording of the last phrase from the King James Version (the one I originally memorized), which reads, "with whom is no variableness, neither shadow of turning" (v. 18). It serves to remind me that though a few of our plans may get gobbled up as we're tumbling along through life, God and His ultimate plan for humanity never change, that everything He ordains is not only for our good but also His greater glory.

So can we train ourselves to see these unexpected interruptions not as banes but blessings? We can if we see each day as a new opportunity to experience God's love, mercy, and faithfulness, even in the midst of unexpected interruptions or affliction.

This was something that took on a very personal significance for Jim and me just last year when, on the last night of a visit from all our kids and grandkids, he suddenly began experiencing severe chest pains. A mad dash to the emergency room followed by a battery of tests revealed five blockages. A few days later, he underwent major coronary bypass surgery. This was something which, with absolutely no previous symptoms, came as a complete surprise. Just as surprising, however, was how quickly through those intense days of waiting and the weeks of recovery that followed, our priorities took on a whole new order. Suddenly, all that was really important was faith and family.

In retrospect we also realize how gracious God was in protecting him and allowing us to discover his heart condition when and how we did. Only a week before, we had taken our kids and grandkids to a local amusement park, and Jim had ridden one of those crazy new roller coasters. What if his heart had acted up then, or three weeks later, when he was scheduled to make a three-day turn-around trip to Guayaquil, Ecuador?

You can be sure Jim has turned his now-requisite two-mile morning walks into prayer walks, always thanking God for the gift of each new day—something that has taken on a whole new meaning for both of us.

This doesn't mean we won't have days of wondering just how far the fabric of our lives can be stretched without tearing. It's on those days we identify most with the words of the weeping prophet, Jeremiah, as they echo across the pages of biblical history—"I remember my affliction and my wandering, the bitterness and the gall. I well remember them, and my soul is downcast within me" (Lam. 3:19).

Seems, though, Jeremiah had already learned the secret of being resilient, even without the benefit of magazine articles and specialists.

"Yet this I call to mind," he continues, "and therefore I have hope: Because of the Lord's great love we are not consumed, for his compassions never fail. They are new every morning; great is your faithfulness. I say to myself, 'The LORD is my portion; therefore I will wait for him'" (vv. 21-24).

Speaking of waiting, I suppose it's only fair to say that, just like those mysterious missing socks, we'll all encounter a number of spiritual struggles here on earth that we'll never understand until we get to heaven. Can't you just imagine walking through heaven's gates and finding a big ol' heavenly sock pile not far down the path? My guess is there'll be a great multitude of newly arrived heavenly hosts gathered round about saying, "So that's what happened to that missing sock!" No doubt we're going to discover a lot of "sole" mates when we get there.

SORTING THROUGH THE STINKY STUFF

Because of Christ, we give off a sweet scent rising to God, which is recognized by those on the way of salvation—an aroma redolent with life.
—2 Cor. 2:15, TM

Sniff, sniff. Whew! What was that smell? It seemed to be coming from the vicinity of the laundry room, and I feared the worst. Since we lived across the street from a large field, it wouldn't be the first time we had experienced small rodents taking up residence in our garage. Could it be that one had somehow maneuvered its way in between the walls and expired? It surely smelled like it.

Truth was, on the day I first noticed the stench, I didn't have time to do anything about it anyway, even if I could have. It came in the middle of a two-week visit from our kids and grandkids, and we had places to go and things to do. I wasn't about to let a rat in the rafters take me away from time with my now far-flung family.

This also meant that stuff on the home front was piling up fast. It wasn't until a couple of days later that I again had time to sniff around. That's when I spied a clump of clothes belonging to one of the grands lying at the bottom of the stairs, waiting for someone going up.

Guess that would be me, I thought, and scooped it up. Just as I did, something foul and funky fell out. No, it wasn't a rodent. It was a boy's well-worn tennis shoe, but it surely smelled like a dead rat! At least now I knew where the stink was coming from.

Have you ever noticed how long it takes sometimes for us to uncover whatever it is that's stinking up our lives? Maybe it's because, as someone once said, we're "just too busy to get organized." Problem is, the more that piles up, the stinkier things get until at some point we have no choice but to stop ignoring the smell and hoping it will go away. Sometimes, as in the case of the sneaker, it's a relief once we pinpoint the source and discover that it may not prove as difficult to deal with as we thought.

In that same smelly sense, not all stress is bad. Stress can motivate us. Take the deadline for this book, for instance. I've always said that if it weren't for deadlines, I would never accomplish anything. Nothing helps some of us get focused like an assignment and a deadline.

What we sometimes forget is that in life we have both.

It was a famous comedian of the 1940s, Joe E. Lewis, who in a more serious moment said, "You only live once, but if you work it right, once is enough." How can we work it right? By intentionally making margins in our lives for the things that are most important.

So let's dive into the stinky stuff and see how many why-we-don'ts might surface. Perhaps by doing so we can determine whether it's merely a case of making life's loads more manageable or a real need to eliminate some things altogether. One warning: this may be more difficult to determine than you think. Why? Because most of the time we set out in search of one obvious, enormous overload, only to discover that most often it's a series of small things that have piled up over a period of time. In that case, it may take some digging to uncover the odious offenders.

The first thing we must do is acknowledge the smell.

Hard as it may be to believe, many of us are actually living with the impression that there's nothing wrong with our wearisome way of life, that it's even—gasp!—normal. *After all, we tell ourselves, isn't the whole world in a hurry? We're only trying to keep up.*

A few years ago my husband, Jim, was driving home behind a friend of his following a conference they had attended. Overeager to get there, the friend was putting the petal to the metal, and Jim was doing his best to keep up. Though they were both somewhat exceeding the speed limit, the guys were also trying hard not to get run over by the even-faster flow of traffic. As often happens, neither saw the hidden highway patrol car until it was too late. Being the last in the line of traffic, Jim was the unfortunate one who got pulled over. Of course, he was hoping that because he wasn't the only one pushing the limits, he would get off with a warning. Try as he might, however, no amount of explaining or finger-pointing was enough to keep him from getting a ticket.

This story underscores a funny yet too-often-truthful saying that recently came to me via e-mail: *If everything seems to be going well, you've obviously overlooked something.* As long as our lives are moving along and we're not getting run over, we can sometimes successfully ignore or justify the fact that we're pushing the limits. Usually, though, it's only a matter of time until we get caught.

Consider this quote from an online article I recently read by Richard A. Swensen, M.D.

> Margin and overload are opposites. Yet, as we have seen, overload is clearly the majority American experience. From activity overload to choice overload to debt overload to information overload to work overload, we are a piled-on, marginless society. Maximizing everything has, of course, become the American way. We push limits as far as possible. This philosophy has become not only business dogma but also standard operating procedure for nearly every sociologic experience.[1]

When I first read that paragraph, I thought of the

question that has become the mantra of many fast-food restaurants: "Would you like to super-size that?"

"Sure," I sometimes want to answer sarcastically. "Or better yet, why don't I just strap a biggie burger to each hip, since that's where it's going to end up anyway? Hey! Got a syringe? Then I can forget about eating and just shoot the cholesterol right into my veins."

We all know that too much of a good thing can be bad. Yet we're tempted at times to ignore the warnings and push the limits. Often we would prefer not even to know if we've overlooked something. Why? That would mean having to make a sensible decision or deprive ourselves of something we really, really, really want for the sake of our health—physical, mental, financial, or otherwise. It occurs to me that with much of the world looking to the United States as a country wise and well advanced in so many ways, we may not be setting a very good example.

Listen as Dr. Swenson continues: "We spend 10 percent more than we have—whether it be money, time, or energy. We work hard, spend hard, play hard, entertain hard, vacation hard, and crash hard."[2]

Crash hard! Now that *really* stinks. Yet it's sometimes the only way we'll stop long enough to evaluate what put us on the collision course in the first place.

I met Carol (not her actual name) at a recent women's retreat. Slim, energetic, and athletic, dressed in jogging suit and sneakers, she's the epitome of the young, mobile mom —except that her tired eyes belied her.

Meeting at my book table, we chatted for a few minutes when an interesting bit of information emerged. "I almost didn't come to the retreat," she said softly. "I've just climbed out of a dark emotional valley and didn't even feel like making the effort, but my husband thought it might do me some good." Sensing there were more details behind her quiet desperation, we made an appointment to meet after lunch and talk further.

Besides being a mom, I came to discover that Carol is also a pastor's wife and a part-time teacher, a job she initially loved but has now come to despise. "It's not the job itself," she explained, "but a lot of other factors that have recently come into play."

Seems after serving a string of small churches and struggling financially through the early years of their marriage and ministry, things had finally taken a positive turn after Carol's husband accepted a staff position at a fairly large church. By this time their three children were in school and involved in a number of extracurricular activities. Though happy up until this time to be a stay-at-home mom, it was then Carol decided to take the part-time teaching position in order to help purchase their first home.

For three years Carol enjoyed the personal fulfillment she found in her job, one that, along with classroom duties, also involved working with music, something she loved. Though busy, she felt she was balancing her random responsibilities well. Then her daughter began having problems in school resulting from some inherited special needs, including attention deficit disorder and another complicated learning disorder. Now these problems were making it difficult for her to advance in a traditional classroom. That's when Carol decided it was in her daughter's best interest to homeschool.

Here's where she also made an all-too-familiar mistake, by overestimating her ability to add one more responsibility without removing something else. She heaped the onus of her daughter's education on top of her already-overflowing plate. This included a major annual children's musical that had become a highlight of the community. When for various unrelated reasons some of her previous parent helpers began dropping out, Carol took on their tasks, too, rather than soliciting more outside resources.

It had now been four years since her decision to homeschool, and the stress was taking its toll. Is it any wonder that shortly before the time of the retreat, Carol had reached a point of being completely overwhelmed by the time challenges and lack of margin in her many responsibilities? Add to that the guilt of failure because she felt she was no longer living up to her own expectations and the expectations of others, plus the realization that she was neglecting her husband and two younger children because of the escalating demands of her daughter's homeschooling.

That's when the anxiety attacks began and depression moved in.

Seeing her so affected, her husband pitched in at home and wisely counseled her to make whatever changes she felt necessary to alleviate the stress. Men often don't understand that with women it's not that easy. As a general rule, a man's almost automatic nature is to compartmentalize. Women are sorters. There's a process we must go through to assure ourselves that we're not hurting or disappointing the people we care about the most by making a decision to do something differently for our own sakes. Woman is our name—nurturing is our game.

What Carol needed most was another woman, someone completely unconnected to her situation, to take the time to listen, then tell her she was not being a bad mother, wife, teacher, or pastor's wife because she desperately needed to rearrange or relinquish some of her responsibilities. By the end of our conversation, she had verbally sorted through her situation and pretty-much come to her own conclusion. She needed to stop adding responsibilities without subtracting others, learn to ask for help, and find a way to meet her daughter's needs that were less draining on her personally.

As usual, God was already there, holding the air freshener. Turns out she had already been offered another teaching position at a different Christian school, one that would not only provide discounts to her two high school children but also allow her daughter to be integrated back into a mainline classroom geared to meet her special needs. An additional perk was a top-notch sports program for her son. Initially, fearing her daughter wasn't yet ready and entertaining some qualms about her own qualifications, she had turned it down. Now that the air was clearer, she realized that this was indeed a door the Lord had opened, and she determined she would revisit it.

We prayed together for His direction and provision. Though it still meant she would have to finish the school year in her current situation, just seeing the end of her dark tunnel of indecision made an amazing difference in her outlook.

Interesting, isn't it, how often we would rather stay in a stressful situation than face the fear of failure or the uncertainty of change? Undoubtedly the thing that makes sorting things out so difficult is that most of our decisions involve people. We can eliminate things, but it may take a little more practice to learn to diffuse people.

This brings us to another important question. It's so hard for us, when someone tries to lay his or her difficulties or additional responsibilities on us, to say "I have all I can handle—I need to ask you to take care of this one yourself." Whether it's the husband who impulsively and repeatedly invites people over and expects his wife to cook and entertain on short notice, the plethora of church programs recruiting new leaders or requiring our attendance at every event, or demanding relatives or friends who consistently burden us with problems and expect us to come up with a solution—because we can't bring ourselves to say no, how often do we find ourselves placed unwillingly or unknowingly in positions or situations we're ill-suited to fill?

No doubt it's because as Christians we don't want to

appear rude, selfish, or uncaring. We would rather be dishonest. Sometimes we even find ourselves apologizing for not making other people's stress our own.

For our own good, what we need to do is learn to be honest, direct, and firm. Like Carol, we need to come to the realization that people can make us do only what we allow them to.

One of the things that may help is learning to return stress to its rightful owner. If we really don't want to do something, we should say so clearly. "I wish I could help, but I just can't do it." That statement leaves little room for negotiation, and you don't want to leave room.

There's nothing wrong with being honest. Returning stress to its rightful owner doesn't mean ducking your own work or avoiding unpleasant tasks. If you have difficulty deciding what your obligation really is, try defining the problem by asking the other person, "Why are you asking me to do this?" The answer will make things very clear to you.

The important thing is that we take positive action before we overreact. For our own good and the good of others, we must find a way to deal with the situation before it gets to the boil-over or melt-down point. Exploding or imploding in the face of stress not only creates more problems but also indicates we have a bigger one than we realized.

Some of our stress is undoubtedly the result of habits that are hard to break. Perhaps we've gotten in such a routine of rushing that we forget the slow lane is not only still an option but the better part of wisdom. "It makes little difference how fast you are in the 100 meters," says author Gordon MacDonald, "when the race is 400 meters long." The writer to the Hebrews talks, too, about running the race with perseverance, but notice he never said anything about speed. In fact, he instructed us to keep our eyes on Jesus "so that you will not grow weary and lose heart" (Heb. 12:3). Obviously there's something to be said for learning to pace ourselves.

But how?

Let's hear again from the good doctor. "The pace of life has become deadly," Doc Swenson states. "We simply cannot permit each year to bring a five-percent increase in speed and not get caught in the exhausting consequences of such frenzy. The green pastures and still waters are awaiting us—but not in the direction the treadmill is spinning."

It's time to stop, turn around, and take a pastoral pause.

He goes on to say that there are two roads leading in the margin direction, one being radical change, the other incremental. While he advises the first as getting us there the quickest, he warns against making any major restructuring decisions—such as cutting work hours, getting a different job, buying a smaller house, relocating to another state or country, or selling expensive luxury items—on impulse. Really radical changes require a longer deliberation period.

On the other hand, he cautions that incremental revisions may not accomplish enough substantive change to make a noticeable difference. His recommendation is that we should try to live more intentionally. "If the world pushes, push back. Practically speaking, there are ways to avoid overload and cultivate margins within the framework of God's design for our lives and ministries."

My mother wasn't a doctor, but she was pretty good at dispensing pills of wisdom. One of the things she often said was "Whatever bothers you the worst, do it first."

When you think about it that way, there are a lot of small sources of stress that we can easily eliminate. In some cases we may have to do it only once; in others, it requires periodic purging.

Take noise pollution. I love my family, but they are noise junkies. Seems the first thing they want to do when they get up in the morning or walk in the door at night is turn something on, usually the television set or CD player. While there are times I, too, enjoy watching a favorite television program or listening to some soothing (the operative word) music, background noise as a general rule drives me nuts. Yet often, after everyone leaves the house, I find myself puttering around, not even noticing the noise emanating from these high-tech troublemakers. Finally I come to my senses and turn them off. Ahh—what a relief! I hadn't even realized how much that constant background buzz was bugging me.

Then there are the clutter culprits that lurk in the open or less obtrusive places in our homes—spots like desks, closets, drawers, and tabletops, anyplace where objects seem to magnetically migrate. For weeks and months I continue shuffling through the stacks, trying to find important papers or jamming back the stuff that falls out of the hall closet every time I open it, rather than taking the time to clean them out. Once I do, the gratification is so great I wonder why I put it off so long.

Perhaps the reason we procrastinate is that it seems like such an overwhelming task. The key, according to cleaning experts, is to break the big jobs down into bite-sized pieces. For instance, don't tackle the whole kitchen or closet—just one shelf or drawer. Dive into a different drawer every day, and in a week's time or so, you will have cleaned them all. Maybe you'll even uncover all those gadgets and appliances you bought over the years that were designed to save time. The trick, then, is not to immediately run out and replace all the items we just tossed with new ones.

What about the predictably stressful situations that we could often avoid with a little prior planning, like standing in long lines at the supermarket or driving in heavy traffic? Yet how many times do we hit the highway at rush hour or dash to the store at dinnertime because we didn't think sooner about where we needed to go or what we needed to buy?

Suppose we suddenly find ourselves with some extra time on our hands. *Hey, we think, now I can get more involved at my child's school. I'll volunteer for president of PTA.* That's great, until the next year when an unexpected financial crunch necessitates our taking a part-time job. So we sensibly resign our position on the PTA, right? No. Most often we keep right on trying to work, run the PTA, and any rash of other responsibilities that may have attached themselves along the way.

Ever wonder if anxiety is hereditary? It certainly might be if we don't use wisdom in helping our children set their own healthy time and emotional limits. When our children observe us taking on too much, then living in a state of illness and anxiety, it can't be a good example for them. We must also use wisdom in the number of extracurricular activities we allow or encourage them to participate in as well as monitor the stress they may experience from overzealous coaches and team parents. The syndrome of the overscheduled and overwhelmed child is becoming much too prevalent in our society.

Now we come down to the most important reason for sorting things out and making space in our lives. "Seek first his kingdom and his righteousness," Jesus says in Matt. 6:33, "and all these things will be given to you as well." What things? The passage goes on to list the basics, like clothing, food, and water.

Funny, Lord. I have a lot more stuff on my to-do list than that.

Ah, but there's more.

"Therefore do not worry about tomorrow, for tomorrow will worry about itself. Each day has enough trouble of its own" (Matt. 6:34).

It seems somewhere along the line we've gotten things a bit backwards. Could it be that much of our daily stress comes from spending too much time today seeking the "tomorrow" things, that in striving to make a better future for ourselves, we're missing some immediate and amazing opportunities? Rose Kennedy, with her hard-won wisdom, said, "Life is not a matter of milestones but of moments." Still we continue to spend the majority of our time seeking things, hoping somehow there'll be time afterward for adding on His kingdom and righteousness.

That's not to say we shouldn't plan for our own or our family's future financial, educational, and health needs. We must keep in mind, though, that no matter how well we work the plan, God grants us only a certain—or uncertain —number of days to use and enjoy what we've been given.

Reflective of the suspected rodent problem mentioned at the beginning of this chapter, consider an appropriate quote from comedian Lily Tomlin: "The trouble with the rat race is that even if you win, you're still a rat."

You may be a modern-day Martha who still needs convincing. Keep reminding yourself that you really are doing this for others. By having less to do—and dust—you'll actually have more time to spend with the people and the Lord you love.

The bottom line is that for our own sakes, the sake of our families, and the service of the Lord, we must start saying no to some of the constant requests and demands. Sniffing out the most common culprits will help us get rid of many stinky sources of stress. In the process, we may also discover that, life-wise, our whites will be whiter, our brights brighter, and our relationships sweeter.

HEAVENLY HAND-ME-DOWNS

As God's chosen people, holy and dearly loved,
clothe yourselves with compassion, kindness, humility, gentleness and patience.
—Col. 3:12

There's no other way to put it—my friend Robin is a neatnik.

I'll never forget my first visit to the well-appointed high-rise condominium she and her husband, Lary (that really is the correct spelling of his name), occupy in San Francisco's famous financial district. From the balcony one can catch glittering glimpses of not only the Pacific Ocean and Bay Bridge but also the seemingly never-ending stream of clientele and cars bustling below.

IT ALL COMES OUT IN THE WASH

Mesmerizing as that all is, the meticulous care Robin has taken in decorating the inside of her home—with its carefully chosen colors, fabulously rich fabrics, and shining glass and chrome fixtures—was equally impressive. Even more than the creamy crown molding, though, the crowning touch for me was the inside of her closets. Everything in there, and I do mean *everything*, has its own personally labeled box, basket, or bin.

People who are that organized amaze me. The only things that have labels in my house are the canned goods, and good luck on finding an uncluttered, much less shiny, surface. Admittedly, my style of decorating is much more cozy and eclectic. Besides that, from bears to heirlooms, I'm a chronic collector. That's not to say my house isn't clean or that Robin's isn't comfy. It's just a difference in personality, style preference, and lifestyle.

Indulge me one more story that humorously describes the difference in our personalities.

Robin is not only a long-time friend—she's also a licensed marriage and family counselor and ministry cohort. As such, a few years ago my husband and I made arrangements to connect with her on an overseas trip to visit pastors and conduct church services throughout England. It so happened that my birthday coincided with this trip. In order to celebrate, we made plans to spend an evening in London for dinner, followed by a live theatre performance.

Arriving early that day, we did a bit of sightseeing and then decided we would squeeze in one last stop at the world famous Harrods department store, a place I had never been. By the time we had hailed a cab and weaved our way through the rush hour traffic, my husband took one look at his watch and announced that we had exactly 20 minutes to shop if we were to make it to dinner and the theatre on time.

Twenty minutes! In this multi-story, block-long icon of the English economic community? He had to be kidding. With no time to waste, Robin, ever the organizer, dashed for the stationery department to purchase a new Day-Timer. I shot off to the souvenir shop.

What is it that makes people so different, or as I prefer to think of it, unique? Much of who we are and what makes us tick come from things I like to call the "heavenly hand-me-downs." First there are the inherited traits and characteristics. These are what distinguish us—make us appear, act, even think differently from others.

Ever notice how early in life a child's personality pops out? Still, it sometimes takes a while for us to figure out that this particular hand-me-down is cut from some pretty interesting cloth. Though I have a personal aversion to putting people in boxes, I'm willing to concede the common conclusion that there are four basic personality types. The type-A *cholerics* are the ones wearing permanent press, meaning set in their ways, somewhat unyielding, and (sorry!) often a bit argumentative. Not surprising since nine times out of ten they're right. In an ongoing effort to please, the cheerful though sometimes insecure *sanguines* may don many different designer duds, but the predominant color will be red in hopes of conveying confidence. The ones who end up in spandex are the *phlegmatics*, "phlexible" and easily able to adjust—often to a fault. Then there are the ever-reflective *melancholies*, whose striving for often-unattainable ideals leaves them disappointed, discouraged, and grieving in basic black.

What about our physical characteristics? Especially in the area of body build and looks, heredity may be something over which we have little control. All I can say to this is thank goodness for cosmetics, calorie-counting, and loose-fitting clothing. Unfortunately, though, while positively altering our outward appearance makes us look better, thus improving self-esteem, it often has little effect on how we see ourselves inside.

Then there are environmental factors such as the home in which we grew up and the way we were taught. These hand-me-downs are embellished with the examples and input of those who have carried significant influence in our lives, such as family members, friends, and mentors.

Add to that our collective cultural climates. Those who were raised in a country the size of the United States or Canada understand how much the place we grew up geographically may have affected our upbringing. For instance, someone growing up in the Deep South of the United States is going to have different traditions, customs, and favorite foods—not to mention a definite drawl—from someone who grew up in the Northeastern or Midwestern states. For those born or raised in other countries, the cultural differences may be even more pronounced.

Whatever the case, one who has suffered deprivation or damage as a child will certainly don a different outlook on life than one who enjoyed more perks and privileges.

There's been a long, ongoing controversy over which affects our behavior the most, heredity or environment—a debate commonly referred to as "nature versus nurture." Most psychologists agree that except in the most extreme cases, it's pretty-much an equal part of both. Sometimes, though, it's hard to know.

As an illustration, let's pay one more visit to Robin. During a recent discussion on what makes people develop certain habits or preferences, she reflected that even as a child she always felt a need to have things around her neatly arranged and organized. I asked whether she believed this propensity for propriety was inherited or learned.

"I always thought because my mother was something of a clutterbug," she admited, "that it was what we call in psychological terms a *reaction formation.*" This means developing a coping reaction to something that really bothers you.

"Then," she continueds, "I met my father." Robin's dad had not been part of her life for most of her younger years. When they finally got acquainted, she was amazed to find some striking similarities. "I'll never forget going out into his garage and seeing his tools hanging on a pegboard, neatly arranged in graduating order by size. Admittedly, it made me wonder which came first—the carpenter or the clutterbug."

Then, too, we can't discount the effect personal life lessons had on our formative thinking. The longer we live, the more experiences we have—some good, some bad. Either way, they all teach us something. Our early observations especially contribute to the formulation of certain outlooks and opinions, some even changing our overall attitude about life. Because these are things we can't always control as children, they may indirectly be considered part of our "heavenly hand-me-downs."

Whether your family history was happy or haunting, many things have contributed to the person you've become, not to mention the way you see and do things. We're each a complex combination of characteristics, all cut from different cloth, so to speak. The lifestyle that works for one may not work for another. Just as different fabrics require different cycles, program settings, and temperatures, so do dissimilar people require a variety of handling and care. No wonder it's so important that we take time to examine these "heavenly hand-me-downs" and see how they're fitting.

As an almost-only child (my brother was 14 years older and had left home by the time I was three), I never had to wear hand-me-down clothing. However, as part of a pastoral family living on a limited income for most of their growing-up years, my kids often had clothes given to them. Some were nearly new and nifty, but some, though given with good intention, were worn or ill-fitting.

Likewise, some of our "heavenly hand-me-downs" fit just fine. These are the positive personality traits that serve us well and are often accompanied by warm memories of the much-loved mentors who modeled them for us. Others bring to mind less-than-positive people or circumstances, ones we want desperately to shed as soon as possible. In many cases it can take years before we finally figure out why the cloth is chafing.

This brings us to a commonly contemplated question: just because Aunt Ethel did something a certain way and we look just like her, does that mean we have to act like her too? More important, when it comes to worst-case scenarios, is family history doomed to repeat itself?

Not if we're willing to learn and change. People who grow up in not-so-nurturing circumstances can choose to do things very differently from the example set for them. The story is told of two brothers whose mother died, leaving them to be raised by an abusive, alcoholic father. One of the brothers pulled himself up by his bootstraps, managed to attend college, and eventually went on to be a well-respected attorney. In an unfortunate turn of events, the other brother followed in the father's footsteps and ended up an alcoholic living on skid row.

Some years later, the background story of the two men reached the ears of a local television newsman who decided to do an interview. His first meeting was with the man who had become an alcoholic. When asked what had brought him to his sad state in life, the brother answered belligerently, "Well, what do you expect with a father like mine?"

The interviewer then sought out the one who had become a lawyer. Again the question was asked about what had encouraged him to seek instead a more successful station. "Well," the other brother replied, "what do you expect with a father like mine?"

Raised with the same parent in an identical environment, each brother developed a different determination and perspective on life. One learned from the father's mistakes and rose above his circumstances, while the other resigned himself to taking the same unfortunate road.

We are the only ones who can accurately examine our individually inherited characteristics and environmental experiences, then determine how the hand-me-downs are fitting. The trick is in finding the balance between accepting the intrinsic traits that we may merely not like much but that make us unique, and the notoriously negative influences affecting our lives and relationships with others. In other words, we need to take a closer look at what we've been handed and ask ourselves, "Is this helping or hindering me?"

Undoubtedly, this will require God's help, but with grace on His part and some guts on our own, we can come away with a more accurate idea of who we are, who we are not, and, most important, what He's designing us to be. Let me reemphasize once again that inheriting certain traits and characteristics does not mean we have to cultivate them.

Before hashing through the hereditary hang-ups that reveal who we are, it may help to first determine who we are not. As already discussed, it's easy for us as women to become so immersed in the lives of others that we forget who we are. Let's make it clear right now: Our identity is not determined based solely on the relationship we have with others. You're not your husband, your children, or your job. Neither does the place you live, whether circumstantially or geographically, define who you are personally or spiritually. Circumstances and living conditions can change quickly and unexpectedly. It's important that when they do, you come away knowing who you are apart from those you live with, where you live, and what you're doing.

Another common struggle worth stressing is that neither are we necessarily what others expect us to be or do. If we're not careful, these real or imagined expectations may even put us over the edge.

As a pastor's wife, my friend Teri had a wide range of responsibilities for which she was receiving a small stipend from the church. One night her husband came home to inform her that the board had decided to give her a raise for all she was doing. "My surprise reaction," says Teri, "was to start crying. I knew I deserved the raise, but I felt that if I took the raise, the board would expect more from me than I was already doing." At that moment, she didn't feel she had an ounce more to give.

Here's another example. Without mentioning names or divulging confidential information, Robin told me of a deeply depressed friend who, feeling that no one else in the family was well-enough suited, had spent a good many years as the sole caretaker for her mother. Her deep sense of responsibility caused her life to revolve entirely around doing things and going to places her mother enjoyed—so much that she had completely lost touch with her own needs and personal desires.

In order to help her reclaim her own identity, Robin suggested the following simple exercise, one we might all benefit from. She asked the woman to make a list of 10 things that brought her a sense of relaxation and 10 things that elevated her heart rate or brought a sense of dread. It took several tries before the friend was able to be completely honest and recognize how much of what she was doing had nothing to do with who she was or what she personally enjoyed. Her life was out of balance, contributing greatly to her depression.

If you've lived as long as I have, you've probably clawed through the closet enough times now to figure out what you have to wear in the way of strengths and weaknesses, inherited and otherwise. You may have also come to the realization that there are certain things about yourself that, like a six-year-old's undies, may never get changed. Instead of continuing to beat ourselves up over that, let's see if we can find a way to either peacefully coexist with, or silence, that ever-present inner critic.

As always, the best place to start is by accepting ourselves the way God made us. Not only is this crucial, but it's also scriptural. "I praise you," the psalmist sings to God, "because I am fearfully and wonderfully made; your works are wonderful, I know that full well" (Ps. 139:14).

Regardless of your role in life, there is no one else on earth like you. You are unique. Do you know it? Then celebrate it! Otherwise you put yourself in a position of arguing with Scripture. As a once-popular poster put it, "God loves you—and God don't make no junk."

Here's an amazing enigma. Only when we accept ourselves the way God made us—warts, bumps, and all—can He start changing us. Why? It's the point where we may find ourselves for the first time honestly assessing our true potential, even though it may also mean recognizing our limitations.

Sound like another contradiction? It's not. Let's face it—we're not going to be perfect at everything, but we can be pretty great at a few things when we put all our effort into them. That's where those with perfectionist personalities may need wisdom from above to know when good is good enough and move on. Asking God to help us determine what deserves our full effort in order to further His plan may actually give us the ability to siphon energy out of things that don't matter and put it into what does.

It's amazing, too, how seeing ourselves honestly adjusts our way of looking at other situations and people. "As we grow to accept our uniqueness," states Robert Schuller, pastor emeritus of the Crystal Cathedral in Garden Grove, California, "we learn to respect the uniqueness of others." Believing that God knew exactly what He was doing when He made us and that He loves us unconditionally goes a long way toward helping us accept our own and others'

shortcomings, not to mention overcoming obstacles resulting from an unfortunate upbringing.

Once our eyes find new focus, we may also start to
notice a few holes in our "heavenly hand-me-downs." After
all, isn't it only too easy at times to blame bad behavior on
heritage or upbringing? "I can't help my temper," some say.
"I'm Irish." Others say, "Don't blame me for being sarcas-
tic. I learned it from my mother."

God will allow us to overlook bad behavior for only
so long before He begins using our inherent nature to reveal that change is necessary. That's when we may notice a
warning label sewn someplace in the seams that reads "Requires Special Handling."

These warnings materialize when something in our
nature or inherited habits starts hitting stress points in our
lives, causing them to begin unraveling. Often it's something we're repeatedly doing or saying that starts adversely
affecting our relationship with our husband, children, or
others. Say, for instance, our argumentative nature begins to
hinder our ability to communicate without conflict. Or our
judgmental genes cause us to come across distant and dis-
approving. Perhaps being insecure or too set in our ways is
stunting our spiritual growth by hindering our ability to
make good decisions or admit our mistakes.

These personality faux pas are especially hard to handle when pointed out by others. As Franklin P. Jones humorously puts it, "Honest criticism is only hard to take
when it comes from a relative, a friend, or a stranger." Re-

gardless of how it's brought to our attention, any characteristic that creates conflict or ill will must be changed.

That's when we must lay aside our pride and pray with the psalmist: "Search me, O God, and know my heart; test me and know my anxious thoughts. See if there is any offensive way in me, and lead me in the way everlasting" (Ps. 139:23-24).

As God begins to reveal the areas needing repair, we may even come to recognize behavior that's destructive or out of control. This could require taking more remedial measures like seeking Christian counseling, even joining a support group or rehabilitation program. Whatever the extent of the problem, every successful attempt at taking corrective measures must begin with two things: honest acknowledgment and repentance.

Though the 1987 movie *Moonstruck* is one I might not recommend for its moral message, it's one that both humorously and poignantly characterizes human weakness and the consequences of poor choices in the arena of our complicated human relationships.

The plot weaves together the stories of several different members of an Italian-American family. One is the father, who's having an extramarital affair, presumably motivated by midlife crisis. This is something his wife has been suspecting for some time. Only after being caught in a compromising situation by his daughter does the guilt start getting to him. Still, rather than confessing and asking forgiveness, he sinks further into despair.

Finally the scene comes in which the wife confronts him at the breakfast table in front of the whole family. In stereotypical Italian patriarchal fashion, he stands, bangs his hand on the table, and begins making excuses. "My life is built on nothin'," he sighs, slumping back into his chair.

In angry but even tones, the wife responds, "Your life is *not* built on nothin'." Her next poignant words are tempered by her tears. "Ti Amo," she states softly—*I love you.*

Sometimes it's discouraging, even humbling, to recognize in ourselves less-than-sterling characteristics or qualities. Yet how freeing and healing it can be when we finally gather the courage to confront whatever behavior is running crossways of God's path for our life. Just knowing that He loves us unconditionally—warts, bumps and all—should make it easier. Not only will He forgive us when we ask, but He'll also help us change our character and hone even the worst habits. Those who love us will help us too. "Love," according to 1 Pet. 4:8, "covers over a multitude of sins."

The result of our honest assessment will be a heavenly hand-over as we put on "a garment of praise instead of a spirit of despair" (Isa. 61:3). Even so, we may have to try on a lot of hand-me-downs here before we finally trade them for the glorious garment He's preparing custom-made in our size and shape.

Perhaps you'll find some instruction and encouragement from Col. 3:9-10, 12-14 as written in Eugene Peterson's wonderful translation, *The Message*:

> Don't lie to one another. You're done with that

old life. It's like a filthy set of ill-fitting clothes you've stripped off and put in the fire. Now you're dressed in a new wardrobe. Every item of your new way of life is custom-made by the Creator, with his label on it. All the old fashions are now obsolete. . . .

So, chosen by God for this new life of love, dress in the wardrobe God picked out for you: compassion, kindness, humility, quiet strength, discipline. Be even-tempered, content with second place, quick to forgive an offense. Forgive as quickly and completely as the Master forgave you. And regardless of what else you put on, wear love. It's your basic, all-purpose garment. Never be without it.

Now that's what I call a "Heavenly hand-me-down!"

LEARNING TO WORK THE CONTROLS

The mind controlled by the Spirit is life and peace.
—Rom. 8:6

Diana Newton had made up her mind. After several trips to Sears to drool over the champagne-colored washer and dryer set she had fallen in love with, the bill of sale was now tucked safely in her purse. Delivery was scheduled for the day after tomorrow.

Only a few weeks prior, Diana, her pastor-husband, and two teenage daughters had made yet another major ministry move. This time, however, the entire family agreed that their worn-out washer and dryer had made its last coast-to-coast crossing. "Anyway," her husband added, "you've waited a long time. You deserve these new machines."

Yes, she thought, *I do*. After all, with one daughter in high school and the other in college, didn't she spend almost as much time in the laundry room as she did in the kitchen? That is, when she wasn't at work, cleaning house, buying groceries, spending time with family, or tending to the various responsibilities she had at church.

When delivery day finally arrived, Diana could hardly contain her excitement. She watched as the two workers unloaded the dynamic duo and began to install them. No doubt about it—they were gorgeous, front-loading, guaranteed to be quiet. She—who admittedly had never much liked doing laundry—could hardly wait to get in there and start washing clothes.

Her enthusiasm was short-lived.

About 20 minutes into the installation, one of the workers called to her. "M'am, could we see you for a minute?"

Diana walked to the hallway to find the two men standing next to the laundry room, pointing to the doorway. The machines looked as perfect as she had imagined. There was just one problem: the door wouldn't close. Her beautiful, perfect, champagne-colored machines were too large for the laundry room.

No way! Diana thought. *I want these—no, I deserve these machines! There has to be a way to make this work!*

"Leave them," she told the workers. "I'll have my husband take off the door when he gets home." Unfortunately, her husband didn't consider that an acceptable solution.

"But you said I deserve these machines, and I don't ever ask for anything and—and I want them." Was that whiny voice really hers? "Besides," she said, taking on a more apologetic tone, "I already tried them out. They work great!"

With this revelation, her husband's suggestion was to have the Sears guys return and see if it might work to stack them. It didn't. That's when reality rushed home to roost. Somehow, Diana's meticulous measurements had come up short. Try as she might, no matter how much she wanted this particular pair to fit, she was just going to have to settle for something smaller. The situation was, quite simply, out of her control.

I can feel Diana's pain, can't you? We've all known the disappointment of getting our hearts set on something, then having things not work out the way we had hoped. At that point we've undoubtedly also found ourselves searching the landscape for surrogate solutions. Even if it means taking off a door or tearing down a wall, we're determined to see our plan through.

In the case of such stuff as washers and dryers, it's pretty easy to justify that determination. After all, aren't these things our society considers necessities? No doubt most of us feel deserving of what we see as life's basics. As a result, we've become good at using our ingenuity and influence—not to mention our credit cards—to get what we want. As long as we're sensible, there's nothing wrong with that.

Occasionally, though, the lines between sensibility and obsession become blurred. This is widely witnessed by how the push for possessions in our society has caused many to get their priorities completely out of whack, not to mention digging themselves deeply into debt. Simply stated, we don't always have the discipline, details, or common sense to make the wisest decisions.

How much more so when it comes to spiritual matters!

Ever find yourself in Diana's dilemma spiritually speaking? I have. I'm notorious for over-obligating myself, then having to move heaven—or at least beseech it—to make things work. It's so easy to get carried away with our own plans and desires. Then when things don't work out quite the way we had hoped, we try every way known to woman to manipulate the matter. Only when we come to the end of our limited resources do we realize the problem might be that we didn't take time to properly compare our plan against God's measurements in the first place.

Even then, some of us are reluctant to let go of the controls. Why is that?

Sometimes it's merely a case of making plans before taking time to think things through. Let's be honest—there are a few everyday things that we feel are just too insignificant to run by God first. So we rush right ahead without seeking His sanction, only to discover that sometimes even the smallest, most seemingly simplistic things can end up having raging repercussions. In laundry lingo, it's like tossing our clothes into the washer without first testing the temperature. Only after we discover that everything has shrunk or turned pink do we find ourselves wishing we had taken a bit more time to review the washing instructions. Maybe that's where the term "wishy-washy" came from.

Then there are those of us who just can't keep from turning the knobs. We want to do things our way, and we're going to keep messing with those buttons until we find what we consider to be the right setting. We would never come right out and say that we think we know more than God does about handling the situation, but our actions make it pretty obvious.

Some of us are just plain impatient. God isn't doing things fast enough, so we're going to help Him out. That usually works about as well as my husband, Jim's, first baking experience.

By his own admission, Jim is one of those patience-challenged people. Once as a college student, he got a craving for his mom's applesauce cake and asked her to send the recipe. Following the directions, he meticulously measured and mixed, then poured the batter into the pan. Everything was looking good until the time came for baking. That's when impatience caused him to make a major mistake. Though the recipe clearly stated that it would take 35 minutes for the cake to bake at 300 degrees, logic coupled with hunger convinced him if he set the oven at 450 degrees, the cake should be ready in half the time. The result was a cake crispy on the outside but like mush in the middle.

Being starving students, he and his college buddies ate it anyway, but it sure wasn't the cake he had hoped to replicate. What a difference just a few more minutes at the right setting would have made!

This makes me think how many of our lives are like that cake as well. They look perfect on the outside, but inside they're falling apart. Though our greatest desire is to emulate the character of Christ, we find ourselves instead skipping steps or failing to follow directions.

Truth is, there are many things in life over which we could exert control if we would just stop pushing all the buttons long enough to seek God for patience and the proper setting—something we undoubtedly need to be reminded of on a daily basis.

That's why I keep a ceramic plaque engraved in gold on my bathroom counter where I can read it every morning. The familiar prayer reads, *Lord, grant me the serenity to accept the things I cannot change, courage to change the things I can, and wisdom to know the difference.* Commonly known as the Serenity Prayer of St. Francis, it reminds me that there really is a serenity or peace that comes from recognizing which things in life we can control and which we can't.

Then there's that word *courage.* Gaining control over our lives often requires us to make some concrete and courageous changes. This means hocking some old habits, the ones we've grown as comfortable wearing as an old pair of sweats, and replacing them with some deliberate disciplines. Certainly it requires taking the time we think we don't have to step back and assess our situation, not with our own limited vision but with eyes of the spirit.

That's a big part of the problem. Because we're human, left to our own devices, we simply don't have the spiritual insight to determine what's most important. According to the apostle Paul, the basis of our control issues boils down to an underlying spiritual battle. Writing to the Christians in Rome, he pegs it this way: "Those who live according to the sinful nature have their minds set on what that nature desires; but those who live in accordance with the Spirit have their minds set on what the Spirit desires. The mind of sinful man is death, but the mind controlled by the Spirit is life and peace" (Rom. 8:5-6).

Could it be that on the days when we find ourselves with little peace in our lives, what we need is to go back and check our settings?

Here's another interesting point to ponder. Ever notice how many of our efforts to control have to do with wanting to change others? *Lord, if only these people would change their ways,* we think, *my life would be so much easier.* Oh, the years of frustration I spent trying to make my oldest son tow the spiritual line and getting my husband to see everything the same way I did, only to get hurt and angry when neither of them responded the way I thought they should.

In the case of my son, God finally helped me see that, according to Prov. 22:6, my job was to "train [him] in the way he should go." The part about "he will not depart from it" (KJV) was up to God. Certainly I had done my best to train him. My problem was that I was trying to do God's job as well. I can't describe the peace that came when I was finally able to release him, trusting God to complete the work in his life.

As for my husband and me having different outlooks on life, it turns out that's something that has actually brought much balance in so many areas over the years—a fact that, because I was often bent on having my own way, I was not always wise enough to discern.

Truly, there's only one person we can control—ourselves. That's why I especially like this modified version of the Serenity Prayer that recently came to me by e-mail: "God grant me the serenity to accept the people I cannot change, the courage to change the one I can, and the wisdom to know that it's *me*."

The biggest hurdle most of us have to jump takes the form of wanting our lives to be like the freshly folded shirts from the local laundry—all wrapped in neat little packages with no wrinkles. When things don't work out that way, we can get bent out of shape faster than a linen jacket. Why? Perhaps it's because, just as Diana felt she deserved the new washer and dryer, we believe we're somehow entitled to have things happen a certain way in life.

My husband often says it's a good thing God doesn't give us what we deserve. "The wages of sin is death," Rom. 6:23 reminds us, "but the gift of God is eternal life in

Christ Jesus our Lord." I don't know about you, but I'll take God's gift over what I really deserve any time.

In retrospect, I've come to believe that our circumstances have little to do with getting what we deserve and everything to do with receiving what we need.

When tough times come into our lives, our Heavenly Father is waiting to walk with us through our circumstances. Things of much greater eternal value are at stake, things we don't recognize because we can see only our immediate circumstances. No wonder, like any child with limited understanding, we might question how His decision can possibly be in our best interest.

That's when Rom. 8:28 comes in handy: "We know that in all things God works for the good of those who love him, who have been called according to his purpose." Not only is God still and always in control of every circumstance—He truly does have at heart the best interest of those who love Him. As Ruth Bell Graham puts it, "God is always on the side of the believer."

Undoubtedly, we'll all experience circumstances that cause us to wonder whether the controls are completely broken. Most often these arrive in the form of long-term situations in which it soon becomes apparent that there's not going to be an immediate resolution. It's then we may feel that God has chosen to run us through the wringer and we're being pressed beyond what we can bear.

How long, Lord, we want to know, *before things get better?*

Isn't it good to know that God is not threatened or

angered by our honest questions? Even at that, we must recognize and accept that for His own as-yet-unrevealed purpose, God is asking us to take our hands off the controls and trust Him. Indeed, He may be using that situation to squeeze out all that keeps us from trusting him completely.

One way or another, we'll be forced at some point to recognize our limitations. While we all possess a certain amount of God-given ingenuity, which He expects us to use, there are going to be things we can't fix. When it comes to my washing machine, for instance, I've learned how to remove and unclog the fabric softener dispenser. But when the thermostat dies or the belt breaks, I know it's time to call in a professional.

Remember, though—the worst thing we can do when we call in a professional is to get in the way. We can actually hinder his or her ability to work by interfering. In the same way, the sooner we release the situation to God, the sooner He can make the necessary repairs and begin the restoring process.

Certainly none of us wants to suffer pain or see bad things happen to people we care about. Again, that's when we must ask God for wisdom to know how much is our responsibility and how much is His.

A few years ago my friend Priscilla, whom I mentioned in an earlier chapter, went through a bad time with her adult son. Like most mothers, she was struggling with some guilt and trying to figure out what she could possibly do to make him straighten up and fly right. In frustration, she met with a Christian counselor who gave her these profound words: "Priscilla, it's not your report card." In other words, this was a situation for which her son would be held accountable, not her.

Want to know how really to be in control? Learn to trust the only one who knows exactly which buttons to push. Recognize that God is sovereign and will do what He wants, when He wants. But know this too: Though God's timer may be on a slightly different setting than ours, He's never late.

One last thing: Trusting God may mean we have to settle for less than what we originally thought was necessary, but if we truly trust Him, what we receive will always be more than enough.

You might be interested to hear how Diana came to grips, or perhaps I should say un-grips, with her ill-fitting, champagne-colored circumstances. Here's her conclusion:

"I finally had to stop and ask myself how I had become so consumed with getting what I 'deserved' when I had never before in my life felt that way. Realizing that I had allowed something relatively unimportant to become such a major focus, I felt awful. That's when I decided that the word *deserve* was not a word I wanted associated with me. God is the one deserving of my love, worship, dedication, and honor. Recognizing this made the kind of washing machines I have seem trivial."

Now here's a lady who definitely has her controls in check.

Her comments also serve to remind us that a key to keeping control is learning to pick our battles, realizing that not everything is as important as we sometimes think. If all else fails, we can give our stress the eternity test by asking this question: "How much difference will this really make 10 years from now?"

In summary, learning to work the controls really means learning to let go of our own plans and desires, our ideas of how things should be done, or the way things should turn out, and trusting the ultimate outcome to God. Missionary martyr Jim Elliot said, "He is no fool who gives what he cannot keep to gain that which he cannot lose." In his case, God required him to give his very life. As a result, an entire community of people came to know Christ.

Was it worth it? I believe Jim Elliot would say it was. You see, besides being a missionary, he was also adept with airplances. Who would know better than he that with God at the controls, we never have to worry about a safe landing?

ENERGY-SAVING APPLIANCES

Cast all your anxiety on him because he cares for you.
—1 Pet. 5:7

Now I ask you—in this high-tech age with all its energy-saving appliances, why can't someone come up with a machine that can just wash all our worries away, ideally with a minimum of agitation? Of course, there are a plethora of pills we can pop. Trouble is, we usually feel better only until the effects wear off. Then the same old fears flood back in like a plugged-up drain. When the plug gets pulled, watch out!

Usually this unclogging comes in the form of some stressful circumstance creating a catalyst that swishes the buried sediment to the surface. Or perhaps we simply wake up one morning barely able to muster the energy it takes to get out of bed, much less face what the day ahead holds. Either way, it hits us in the face like a soppy sweatshirt. Something is sucking the life out of us, and we can no longer cope. We won't be going anyplace until we figure out where the leak is.

Ever wonder what women did before the miracle of modern machines? From what I've read and observed, our great-grandmothers did all the chores we do today, plus many more, with none of the conveniences. Yet by some miracle, they still had time left over for leisure activities such as sewing, reading, or socializing. How in the world did they manage that? Perhaps it was because they didn't have as many of our modern options and obligations, like television and after-school soccer.

Still, they had only a modicum of medicines, a trickle of technology, and little choice in limiting the size of their families. When it came to sickness and sacrifice, these long-ago ladies learned to live with a lot. Trusting the Lord was often their only option. Undoubtedly no one understood better than they did a statement made by Maude Royden: "When you have nothing left but God, then for the first time you become aware that God is enough."

What about those who lived during the war years of the early 1900s, followed by the Great Depression? Though technology had advanced somewhat, it was still a time of unparalleled hardship because of economic emergency. It wasn't until World War II rumbled onto the scene that things began to improve in North America both economically and technologically. It also happened that, with most of the men serving in the military, many ladies of that era laid down their ladles and took up their tools, ushering in a new wave of women in the workforce.

One lingering lesson from these turbulent times was that you could not afford to waste anything. "Waste not, want not" was an adage still being impressed on my generation.

Speaking of which, let me lay something to rest. Old sitcoms would have us think that women in the 1950s did nothing but stay at home, cook, and clean. They often portrayed a woman who, sporting the perfect coiffure and flawless cosmetics, wore pearls, a dress, and high heels even when vacuuming.

Judging from memories of my own mom, this is not quite accurate. What I remember as a kid growing up is that we had our "good" clothes—those saved for wearing to school, church, and social functions—and our "old" clothes, for working or lounging around the house.

Actually, during this time many women, my mother included, opted to continue working outside the home. That didn't mean, however, that when they got home their workday was over. There was still dinner to cook, kids to bathe, and the house to clean. Maybe that's the real reason they were vacuuming in heels: they never had time to change clothes. At least by this time they *had* electric vacuum cleaners and a plethora of other power-driven appliances. This not only made life easier but also allowed them to accomplish much more.

Even so, by the time the 1970s rolled around, someone decided that this simply wasn't enough. Women had more to offer than washing and vacuuming. It was time for their roles in society to be transformed. To prove the point, they took to the streets, burning their bras and campaigning for equality. While this gave women a public platform, it didn't do much to reduce stress.

One of the humorous illustrations I use to support this when speaking for women's events is a comic strip I clipped out some years ago featuring the cartoon character Cathy. In it the creator, Cathy Guisewite, uses her pen-and-ink counterpart to humorously depict the societal changes in the role of women over the last 50 years.

The first frame, labeled with the year 1955, shows a woman's arm and hand brandishing a sparkling diamond engagement ring. Its one-item to-do list is captioned "Marry well."

Fast forwarding to 1975, the next frame again shows the woman's arm and hand, this time curled into a fist. It, too, contains a one-item list: "Transform role of women in society."

By 1995, frame number three shows six arms wildly waving items representing a range of random roles and containing a 15-item to-do list. These run the gamut from earning a living, buying a home, marrying, and raising children, to saving the planet and fighting against evil, then going into therapy to regain vulnerability.

The final frame shows Cathy, still in her business suit, prostrate on a couch surrounded by stacks of stuff. The balloon caption reads, "I am woman. Hear me snore."

Needless to say, this always gets a loud laugh and knowing nod from audiences. Seems we new-millennium women are well acquainted with weariness.

According to surveys I've taken at these same retreats, many of my generation—the ones who maneuvered through Mod Podge and macramé while collecting all the time-saving tools they could grab along the way—have still managed to fill up every extra minute they saved. Many of these liberated women are just plain exhausted. While trying to do everything we now have the freedom and society's endorsement to do, we've discovered that we may have let some important things slip. Many women are living with a lot of worry, regret, and guilt.

Not that that's anything new.

Sometimes it's easy to look back and convince ourselves that times were simpler in other generations. Yet I vividly remember my grandmother using phrases like "I'm still stewing over that," or "I've worried that problem to death." Seems anxiety is an area in which women of all generations have always tended to spend too much valuable time and energy.

Let's be honest—no matter how happy a person appears on the outside, no one lives without harboring some hurtful experiences. Whether it's a deep-seeded situation from childhood or grudges accumulated in adulthood, all of us at one time or another struggle with unresolved emotions from the past that are draining our energy and ability to balance our lives today. Sometimes it takes years before we even recognize it.

Why? There are many reasons, but let's look at what I believe are three of the most common.

Seems many of us struggle with the feeling that perhaps we've done something unforgivable. Sure—we know 1 John 1:9 by heart and believe God has forgiven us, that Jesus' blood has permanently bleached away the stain of our sin. What we just can't seem to get rid of is that pesky ring of guilt around the collar.

We're in good company.

No one suffered a more sorrowful sin than David when he committed adultery with Bathsheba, then had her husband, Uriah, killed. Listen to this portion of Ps. 51, which David wrote after being confronted by the prophet Nathan: "Create in me a pure heart, O God, and renew a steadfast spirit within me. Do not cast me from your presence or take your Holy Spirit from me. Restore to me the joy of your salvation and grant me a willing spirit, to sustain me" (vv. 10-12).

David asked for God's forgiveness. Still, it's obvious that he realized a willing spirit would be needed if he was ever to forgive himself and once again find joy. We, too, must be willing to believe God's Word when it says that He has not only forgiven but forgotten our sin. In spite of David's sins and shortcomings, God referred to him as a man after His own heart. Surely there's a special place in God's heart for us as well.

"But you don't understand," you may say. "What I did hurt someone I loved deeply. How can I ever forgive *myself* for that?"

That's energy-zapper number two: the inability to forgive ourselves, often causing us to reside in regret. Believe me—it's a subject with which I'm well acquainted, one that I address in detail in my first book, *Prodigal in the Parsonage: Encouragement for Ministry Leaders Whose Child Rejects Faith*. The book relates my painful journey and the journeys of others with prodigals. In our case, it was a trip spanning several years during which both of my parents passed away. Though we survived the struggles and reconciled most of the regret relating to our children, I carried the guilt for years over having to place my mother in a nursing home during that time rather than caring for her myself. On top of that, within five years of her death, my father was diagnosed with cancer. Though I was able to assist my brother with his care on weekends, my job prevented me from being there the morning he unexpectedly died. Add yet another regret.

These were the two people I loved most in the world, the people who had taken care of *me*. My brother assured me that I had done all humanly possible considering my own situation at the time. Though I knew in my heart that no one would be more understanding or forgiving of my situation than my parents, for years I struggled to shake the feeling that I had let them both down in their hour of greatest need.

Some of my worst guilt trips were taken at night. How many times during those difficult years did I fall into bed exhausted, only to be awake two hours later, all hope of sleep lost? That's when I began to recognize that it was not just a struggle with emotion but a struggle with oppression. Somehow I needed to find a way to keep my mind from traveling the devil's dark and desolate roads.

Taking Jesus' example, I determined to combat the enemy with God's Word. From then on when those sleepless nights came, I quoted scripture or called up melodies from favorite faith and scripture choruses. Some nights, still unable to shake the sadness, I simply said the name of Jesus over and over again.

What a blessing to know that any hour of the day or night we can call on Him! "If you wake me each morning with the sound of your loving voice, I'll go to sleep each night trusting in you" (Ps. 143:8, TM). It was by tuning in to His forgiving voice above all others that I was finally successful in letting the guilt go.

The third equally difficult dilemma we face is the task of forgiving others. We all know how hard it is when we've been hurt or wronged by someone to find it in our heart to forgive—especially if we feel we did nothing to deserve the terrible treatment. Often we're angry. Sometimes we want revenge, or at the very least for the person to come groveling on hands and knees, begging our forgiveness.

Again this was a situation I found myself struggling with when our son was making choices and doing things that hurt us deeply. *How can he be so inconsiderate?* I often found myself thinking. *One of these days he'll be sorry and want our forgiveness.* The attitude-altering day for me came when I knew the Lord was telling me that I needed to forgive him, even before he asked for it. Like removing one too many soggy blankets from an overloaded machine, what a weight was lifted!

Speaking of overload, could it be that some of us continue to carry the pain, anger, guilt, and grief of the past only because we don't know where to drop it? Perhaps it's a case in which we've held onto it for so long that we don't know what we'll replace it with, and we're terrified of the hole it may leave in our heart.

Then, too, acknowledging it means we may have to change, do something differently, or take personal responsibility. We're simply not prepared to do that, or perhaps we don't know how. Again, these deep-seeded issues are ones that may require the help of a Christian counselor to sort out and determine what the best spot-removing treatment or repair remedy might be.

Regardless, when it comes to dealing with these and other difficult life issues, we can always use some scriptural support. The best energy-savers I know are found in Ps. 37: 5-9, a passage of Scripture I quote often:

Commit your way to the LORD; trust in him and he will do this: He will make your righteousness shine like the dawn, the justice of your cause like the noonday sun.

Be still before the LORD and wait patiently for him; do not fret when men succeed in their ways, when they carry out their wicked schemes.

Refrain from anger and turn from wrath; do not fret—it leads only to evil. For evil men will be cut off, but those who hope in the LORD will inherit the land.

In case you missed them, the four energy-savers mentioned in this passage are "commit," "trust," "hope," and "wait." Amazing how these relate right back to some of the very lessons gleaned from past generations, lessons like going to God first instead of trying to work things out on our own. The trick here, of course, is to give it to God and then leave it there. Don't keep trying to take back what you've already committed to Him. As long as you continue to carry the grudges, anger, guilt, and hurt, you can't truly commit these things to the Lord. Not only that, but it could be detrimental to your spiritual health as well. Heed the words of William H. Walton: "To carry a grudge is like being stung to death by one bee."

This brings us to another hard-learned lesson: Waste not, want not. Committing things to God places them in His hands, freeing us so that we no longer waste energy worrying about them. Trusting Him means we're also free from fear of what the future may hold. Surely this allows us to put our energy to better use in fulfilling God's plan in the present.

Corrie ten Boom said, "Worry does not empty tomorrow of its sorrow; it empties today of its strength." As a holocaust survivor, she surely knew. She also understood and wrote much about the unexplainable hope that comes from committing and trusting our lives to Christ, even under the darkest circumstances.

Face it—even with all of our modern technology, when it comes to matters of the heart, there are still some things for which there's no quick fix. Our hope must be in the Lord, and sometimes His timetable is different than ours, which means we must not only trust Him but often wait. In the case of our prodigal son, it took almost 20 years, but the day did eventually come when we heard Him say, "Mom and Dad, I'm really sorry for all the things I did that hurt you. Can you forgive me?" What a joy to be able to say, "We already have." Still, there's no doubt that it was a lesson in patience for all of us.

Some of us are carrying hurts so deep that they may require an inner healing. Often these are circumstances over which we had or have no control. Nor do we have the ability to go back and change them. Still, we spend hundreds of unproductive hours wrestling with the "what ifs" and "if onlys." Whether they take the form of a wayward child, an unfaithful spouse, a disloyal friend, an unexpected crisis, an unwanted change, or issues from the past such as neglect and abuse, these are all things that may take time to resolve but need not drain our daily energy.

"Every tomorrow has two handles," says author Henry Ward Beecher. "We can take hold of it with the handle of anxiety or the handle of faith." The choice is ours. To filter our emotions through faith, even when we don't fully understand them, is the key to a future full of balance and blessing. Conversely, hiding anxiously behind the door only prevents us from stepping through and moving on.

Does that mean we may not occasionally be tempted to revisit some painful places? No—it just means we don't have to stay there. Once we've mastered the technique of applying these energy-saving devices, we'll never want to go back to our old way of doing things again.

TAKING OUT
THE STARCH

Come with me by yourselves to a quiet place and get some rest.
—Mark 6:31

"Ahh, yes! Hoo, boy—does that ever feel good!"

We had just left church and weren't even out of the parking lot before my husband had pulled off his tie and unbuttoned the top button on his shirt. Though the dress code at most churches these days is considerably more casual than it used to be, his position as a denominational executive still dictates that in most cases he wear a suit and tie. In order to keep his dress shirts crisp and uncrinkled, he has the cleaners apply extra starch on the collars and cuffs. Amazing how just loosening that chafing collar seemed to relax his whole demeanor.

If only it were always that easy.

Unfortunately there are those days when he has to stay in "uniform" all day long, sometimes even into the late hours of the evening. Those may be occasions when meetings go long or he's dealing with some difficult issue. Then even an eventual change into his comfiest clothes doesn't always enable him to relinquish the weight of his responsibilities.

Like many, he's one of those guys who takes his role seriously—a little too much at times, as I'm apt to remind him frequently. Not that I'm much better. How often do I find myself up to my neck in my own set of stiff, starchy stress caused by demands and deadlines—much of it, I hate to admit, self-imposed.

Face it—most of us have trouble letting down without feeling guilty about being derelict in our duties. Yet isn't this the very reason we need to take care of ourselves?—so we won't burn out, perhaps depriving people of our presence when it's most important. Following the long tradition of Jewish wit and wisdom, Rabbi Hillel said, "You have a solemn obligation to take care of yourself, because you never know when the world will need you." How quickly, though, that same world can start scratching as it pokes and prods us!

That's why all of us need to step back often and examine our schedules, then determine what we can do—or stop doing—to make time for the things and people in our lives who are most important. Unfortunately, though, our need to hold up under the heat often causes us to just keep spritzing on the starch. Only when we reach a point of physical or emotional exhaustion, or a serious health crisis hits us, are we finally willing to concede that perhaps we should have been taking better care of ourselves. Now that's what I call sticky build-up. Then it's not enough that we simply loosen our collars—it may require a good, long soak if we're ever going to get all the starch out.

What is it about our human nature that often requires either a God-given mandate or a major wake-up call before we become motivated to make changes? We've already established that our lack of balance in this and other areas is usually not just a time management mistake but a spiritual oversight. So maybe it will help to be reminded that not only is rest and relaxation a scriptural principle but also something both God the Father and Son modeled for us as well.

"There remains, then, a Sabbath-rest for the people of God," Heb. 4:9-11 tells us, "for anyone who enters God's rest also rests from his own work, just as God did from his. Let us, therefore, make every effort to enter that rest, so that no one will fall by following their example of disobedience." Many times, too, Scripture records that Jesus either left alone or took His apostles and retreated to wilderness areas to fast, meditate, and pray.

I would say that being the Creator and the Savior of the world are both pretty big jobs, wouldn't you? If He knew when it was time to say either "It is good" or "It is finished" and rest, what in the world makes us think our jobs are any more important?

Suffice it to say, God has made many provisions in His Word for our health and well-being. We can't go against them and expect not to suffer the consequences. We're not talking about taking an annual vacation as much as finding daily ways to make healthful, balanced choices. Take for instance our diet, exercise habits, and sleep patterns.

Uh-oh.

As a general rule when it comes to food, we're an overfed but undernourished society. Simply for the sake of speed or convenience, we choose foods that are not natural, highly processed, and full of all the worst stuff we can possibly put into our bodies. And don't think reading the packaging is going to help much. The people who market these munchies are experts at choosing slogans that make us believe we're picking a more healthful, much-improved product.

Add to this the little amount of exercise the average North American gets, and you have a formula for physical disaster. No wonder our arteries are clogged, our brains blurry, and our circulation shutting down. Often our answer is to go on some unrealistic diet regimen that sends our bodies into metabolic tailspin, sweat just enough to drop a few pounds, then start the cycle of unhealthful eating and couch-potato existence all over again.

Been there, ate that.

No doubt we need to educate ourselves, not only for our own sake but also that of our children. Consider these starchy statistics. The American Medical Association states that heart disease, even beyond breast cancer, is the leading cause of death for women over the age of 50. Also, 65 percent of American children are obese, and diabetes—both childhood and adult-onset—has become a modern-day epidemic.

As for sleep, we can't seem to get everything done during the daylight hours, so we burn the candle at both ends, often for days at a time. Here's a place I must also admit guilt. Being a night person, I'm notorious for rarely getting to bed much before midnight. *It doesn't matter,* I'm prone to think, *as long as I still get six or seven hours of sleep, right?* At a recent workshop, I got a real wake-up call when it comes to sleep. I heard from someone there that the hours of sleep we get before midnight actually count *double.* If that's true, I think I'm in double trouble.

What about the nights when we get to bed at a reasonable hour only for our infernal, internal time clocks or some nagging neurosis to steal our sleep? Or perhaps it's some negative emotion such as anger, guilt, or grief that comes to call. I've heard that emotions gone awry can even release toxins into our systems and make us sick.

For years I thought I was the only one who suffered from an almost unrelenting 3 A.M. wake-up call. That's the tremulous time when everything seems more magnified and malicious. Then, at a writer's conference, I heard Bar-

bara Hudson Powers recite her poem entitled "God of
Three A.M." and knew that neither of us was alone. See if it
rings a bell for you.

> *Dear God,*
> *Are you God of 3 A.M.?*
> *When all the greepies*
> *and groolies and growlies*
> *come out, shadows shout,*
> *and I doubt?*
> *When I weep*
> *and cannot sleep?*
> *Are you God of 3 A.M.?*
> *I know you're God of morning hours*
> *when butterflies minuet on flowers.*
> *I know you're God of noontime bright,*
> *when the way is clear and all seems right.*
> *I know you're God of evening hours*
> *when rainbows shimmer after showers.*
> *But are you God of 3 A.M.?*
> *When all the greepies, and groolies,*
> *and growlies come out,*
> *shadows shout and I doubt?*
> *When I weep and cannot sleep?*
> *You are.*
> *"The Lord is my shepherd*
> *I shall not want."*
> *I say the twenty-third Psalm*
> *over and over again.*

Sleep comes. Shadows go.
The morning light is fair and bright.
You are God of peace and power.
You are God of every hour.
*You are God of 3 A.M.**

Counting on the Good Shepherd, it seems, is even better than counting sheep. Ps. 121:1-3 says, "I lift up my eyes to the hills—where does my help come from? My help comes from the LORD, the Maker of heaven and earth. He will not let your foot slip—he who watches over you will not slumber." The way I see it, if the Lord's up anyway, there's no point in both of us losing sleep.

The best motivation for making these challenging changes in our health habits is to be reminded who our bodies belong to, something Paul addresses in 1 Cor. 6:19-20: "Do you not know that your body is a temple of the Holy Spirit, who is in you, whom you have received from God? You are not your own; you were bought at a price. Therefore honor God with your body." Obviously we and the Corinthians weren't the only saints struggling. Paul writes to the Romans as well: "I urge you . . . in view of God's mercy, to offer your bodies as living sacrifices, holy and pleasing to God—this is your spiritual act of worship" (Rom. 12:1).

American women today are living well into their 80s, which means longer life spans and added potential for ex-

*Barbara Hudson Powers, "God of Three A.M.," Box 3722, Thousand Oaks, CA 91362, © 1956. Used by permission.

tended ministry. Let's not be like the elderly lady who said, "If I'd known I was going to live this long, I'd have taken better care of myself." No doubt every laundry room can accumulate some toxic trash. It doesn't take much time to identify what may be potentially hazardous to our health and do a clean sweep.

Here's something else I've noticed. Taking control over our physical disciplines not only makes us feel better, it also causes us to want to bring our spiritual disciplines into balance. Somehow the two are often related. Or is it the other way around?

Now let's take a closer look at the cobwebs in the corners. Some of the stiffest competitions we encounter when it comes to taking out the starch are from things that are much less obvious. Take lowering our expectations, for instance.

My good friend and book-writing buddy Laura Jensen Walker discovered that as her writing career took on full-time status, she had to make some major concessions in this area in order to meet her all-important publishing deadlines. Obviously this required learning to say no and not being as accessible as she once was. One practical way she found to do this was not to answer the phone while she was writing, letting the answering machine pick it up instead. Sound easy? Not when you're given to grabbing the receiver every time it rings or afraid of missing some important message. More likely what you'll miss will be a few marketing calls, in which case I would say it's worth the chance.

She also had to learn to live with a messy house, at

least during the last three or four weeks before her deadline. "This was difficult for me," she states, "since my mom was the self-proclaimed Queen of Clean."

She managed to master both, though, carving out not only the much-needed time for creativity but also room for replenishing her inner resources as well. Once, with relatives due to arrive right on the tail of one draining deadline, she even treated herself by hiring a cleaning lady to come in for a few hours. "My house looked great," says Laura, "and for once I wasn't too wiped out to visit and have fun with my relatives." This is no easy task for those of us who feel we have to clean before the cleaning lady comes.

One more way Laura learned to let down was to lighten up when it came to impressing people with her culinary skills. "I love to have friends over for tea," she says, "a full-on English one complete with china, dainty sandwiches, savory treats, scones, and yummy desserts—things that could easily take a whole day to prepare." Now she usually makes up just one kind of sandwich, then visits the specialty aisle of her local store for the other items. "I still set a beautiful table and serve my guests wonderful food—it's just made by others. The important thing is that I get to spend time with them rather than in the kitchen."

Cheerio, old girl!

Speaking of deadlines, ever realize how many of those little suckers are self-imposed? A recent e-mail from my counselor friend Robin gives a great illustration as well as a super suggestion.

"Even on the days when I have no clients," she writes," I wake up in the morning with deadlines in my head. Things like 'I have got to get that already-late birthday gift off today' or 'I need to set up an appointment to get my contacts changed . . . run a couple of loads of laundry . . . make a special dinner for my husband since he's working late . . . clear my overflowing e-mail inbox—on and on it goes. Before I know it, my day is full of deadlines.

"The problem is that the past several days have been long ones with even longer nights full of deadlines. Though I'm not sick or on my period and even had a full nine hours of sleep, I'm groggy, cranky, and basically non-energetic. My body, which does not lie, is telling me it's time for an ND—meaning non-deadline—day."

Here's Robin's way of creating an ND day. She absolutely does not get dressed until after noon. "Something about staying in my robe keeps me in the relaxation mode," she says. "It reminds me that I'm not being a professional today, not going out and about to accomplish any to-do list."

She goes on: "Many things in my world are not optional and are time-sensitive, needing to happen by a certain deadline; but many are things that others would have me make happen according to their schedules. On an ND day, those are the things I put on hold or say no to doing."

Other things that help us create an ND day are choosing to do only things we feel like doing. If it's early November, we might feel like doing some Christmas shopping. We might feel like calling a friend for a long chat. We might decide we're in the mood to clean out a pantry or bake some cookies. On the other hand, it might be a great day to cuddle up with some popcorn and soda and tune in that old movie we've been wanting to watch.

"It's the delicious option," says Robin, "of doing whatever you're in the mood to do, even if it's a bubble bath at 2 P.M." She's quick to add that creating an ND day doesn't mean we're not productive. It simply means there are no time pressures, no demands, and nobody else's deadlines to juggle. The rest of the week may be full of committee meetings, clients, and picking up the cleaning, yet it's amazing how one ND day will restore the energy and enthusiasm for doing everything else with joy."

The counselor in her concludes, "It's a basic and foundational piece God has given us for arranging our lives—a day of rest from the deadlines we impose on ourselves and that others lovingly demand or need from us. I invite you to consider an ND day every so often and see how genuinely healing it can be for you."

I can already hear some of you major Marthas wondering, *How in the world would I ever manage to take a whole day off without feeling guilty?* Just take to heart the old saying "Prevention is worth a pound of cure." By giving ourselves a guilt-free break, we may actually be avoiding future breakdown.

Speaking of giving ourselves a break, what about the fact that everyone has a bad day every now and then? Sometimes the best thing to do when that happens is accept it and go with the flow. It's also entirely possible that somewhere down the line we're going to do something just plain dumb. When that happens, the only healthy thing to do is learn to laugh at ourselves instead of being our own toughest critic. As an exaggerated illustration, here's one of my favorite funny stories.

Seems a rather well-proportioned secretary, Joan, spent almost all of her vacation sunbathing on the roof of her hotel. She wore a bathing suit the first day, but on the second she decided that no one could see her way up there and slipped out of it for an overall tan.

She had hardly begun when she heard someone running up the stairs. Since she was lying on her stomach, she just pulled a towel over her backside.

"Excuse me, Miss," said the flustered little assistant manager of the hotel, out of breath from running up the stairs. "The hotel doesn't mind you sunbathing on the roof, but we would very much appreciate your wearing a bathing suit as you did yesterday."

"What difference does it make?" Joan asked rather calmly. "No one can see me up here, and, besides, I'm covered with a towel."

"Not exactly," said the embarrassed little man. "You're lying on the dining room skylight."

See? Laughter really is still the best medicine.

If you can't carve out an entire day, at least consider some smaller segment of time. Learn to take "five-minute vacations." When it's impossible to remove all stress from your environment, remove yourself. Slip away. Take a walk. Enjoy the solitude, fresh air, and freedom from stress. Even if it only brings temporary relief, it may be enough to give you a fresh perspective on finding solutions to problems.

Take time out to play. Famous playwright George Bernard Shaw said, "We don't stop playing because we grow old; we grow old because we stop playing."

Here's how that same lesson sounds in Greek.

Greek legend tells us that in ancient Athens a man noticed the great storyteller, Aesop, playing games with some children. The observer laughed at Aesop for this undignified behavior. Instead of replying, Aesop picked up a bow that he sometimes used for playing a stringed instrument, unstrung it, and laid it on the ground. "Now answer this riddle," he said to his critic, "and tell us what the unstrained bow implies." The man could not tell him, so Aesop explained. "If you keep a bow always bent, it will break eventually; but if you let it go slack, it will be more fit for use when you want it."

It's like that with people too. That's why we need to take time to rest—maybe even to play a few childish games.

"The need for solitude and quietness," author A. W. Tozer wrote, "was never greater than it is today." Make a quiet space in your home, be it an entire room or just an out-of-the-way corner. Furnish it with a comfy chair, favorite books, and whatever else brings you peace of mind. My friend Marla uses a sunny spot near a window in her living room, complete with a big basket containing all the components for her daily devotions. It's also a great place to read or journal.

Journaling, by the way, is one of the best methods I know of releasing emotion and gaining perspective. Putting feelings on paper clears our mind. Something about seeing our thoughts in writing clarifies them. As well, reflecting back on what we've written helps us see how far we've come. That can't help but bring balance.

Keep a clip file, too, of articles that encourage or bring a sense of serenity. The following paragraph was actually a lead-in for an article on different types of bedspreads. It contained such a calming word picture that I kept it for future reflection.

There is a brief moment, as the bed linens are being changed, when a summer spread assumes the grace of a parachute. Suspended in midair, hovering and billowing, the cloth pauses before floating down to the mattress in slow motion. It's just a ritual, this changing of linens. A custom. But like the first sweet smells of cut grass and fresh rain, it awakens the senses; in a moment or two, it makes the bedroom appear brighter, airy, and inviting.

Ahh.

There are no better mental images than those found in Scripture and none creating a more peaceful portrait of tranquility than the 23rd Psalm. Certainly no one knew more about stress than its author, King David. My guess is that as things heated up in the palace, David spent a fair amount of time reflecting on the cool green pastures of his previous, less stressful position as a shepherd. Looking for a restful retreat? Consider taking a few minutes right now to dangle your feet in those quiet waters.

Don't think, though, that "restful" means "easily un-raveled." From that simplest of settings come some of the most profound principles in Scripture.

A little boy was once asked to memorize Psalm 23 but had trouble remembering all the lines. When the time came to recite it, he was reluctant. The teacher encouraged him just to do the best he could.

"The Lord is my shepherd," he began, then hesitated. "The Lord is my shepherd," he repeated, but could get no further. Glancing nervously at his teacher, he suddenly remembered her admonition. "The Lord is my shepherd," he quoted boldly, "and that's all I need to know."

When it comes right down to it, taking the starch out of our lives is bound to be an ongoing challenge. Somehow, knowing that the green pastures and still waters are only a stone's throw away helps. The Lord is our shepherd. Maybe in that end that's all we, too, really need to know.

THE
IRONING BASKET

Being confident of this, that he who began a good work in you will carry it on to completion until the day of Christ Jesus.
—Phil. 1:6

Even in today's world of wash-and-wear, some of us still have one—a basket where we toss the things that need to be ironed out. Sometimes we don't look in there for weeks—maybe months. By the time we do, we're often surprised at what we find. Depending on how long it's been, some of the garments may have even gone out of style or no longer fit. There'll always be a few things, though, that we're delighted to discover—a favorite forgotten blouse, perhaps, or the sweater we tossed in by mistake and thought was lost.

The same could surely be said of our hopes, dreams, and desires.

Face it—the deeper we find ourselves dug into the trenches of everyday living, the more likely something's going to get buried. Even in our enlightened Western culture, it's not uncommon that women are still most often the ones who end up sacrificing their own interests for the sake of others, usually their husband's or children's. Sometimes it's that old nurturing nature that kicks in, causing us to believe that everyone else's gifts or opportunities are more important than our own. More often, though, it's simply the practical matter of not having enough time or financial resources for everyone to do what he or she would like, so we defer.

Either way, before we know it, the desires of our once-hopeful hearts become buried, our secret longings left to languish, neglected or forgotten at the bottom of life's brimming basket. Every so often we may find ourselves wondering what ever happened to this idea or that, or how different life might be had we made other choices. One warning, though: Allowing ourselves to dwell on this too long may issue an open invitation to underlying resentment, an unwanted guest we don't want to take up residence.

As mentioned earlier, feeling out of control of our circumstances or powerless to pursue our passion may open the door to depression. I remind you once more that those who trust in the Lord are never out of control or powerless.

The important thing is that as we're waiting for circumstances to change or develop we not give up hope and forget or minimize the unique gifts, talents, and abilities we possess, or the plans we once wanted so much to pursue. When life's ironing basket overflows, it's often the dream of what waits just beneath the surface of our everyday duties that keeps us going.

I've observed that there's more than one good underlying reason we sometimes have to wait for these things to come to fruition. Perhaps it's a matter of first getting our priorities in order and our lives in balance. More likely, however, is the fact that though we may possess the talent and might even be presented with the opportunity to pursue any number of interesting options at an early age, we don't yet have the maturity needed for what may accompany them. Face it—the only thing worse than feeling your desire has been lost or overlooked is to jump into something prematurely and fail utterly. God's timing is always of the utmost importance.

Know this too. In God's economy nothing is wasted. Those He calls He also equips. What we discover is that through the years we may actually have been entertaining a calling within a calling, that through the everyday circumstances of our lives God has been preparing us, almost without our even knowing it.

For as long as I can remember, I've had a love affair with words. When I was a kid, one of my favorite games on long trips was to have my mother give me words to spell. From an early age I kept a daily diary; then, starting in the sixth grade, I did stints on several school newspapers. Even after marrying and entering full-time ministry, I kept writing for my own enjoyment, often as an emotional outlet. Along the way, I composed poems and plays for a number of major church events. For years my greatest creative endeavor was an annual newsletter, mailed to family and friends who often responded with kindness and encouragement. Though at the time I had no serious ambitions about ever being published, two of my first published pieces were ones written during those years.

Was the fact that I excelled in English and chose secretarial training as a vocation in high school an accident? Looking back, I can see how God was leading me in the direction of my gifting, even providing me with basic grammar and composition training. Still, it would be years before the opportunity for publication was presented.

Here's one more observation that may be an encouragement. While many men pursue only one main vocation or interest in life, women tend to have many. I believe it has to do with the fact that, for a variety of reasons, it takes most women a while to see themselves as independent individuals, capable of making sound decisions. Many marry young, transferring their dependence from their parents onto their husbands. Some, whether single or married, pursue careers, but their biological bifocals cause them to focus on marriage, homemaking, and childbearing as their primary purpose. Therefore, the jobs they take during this time may not necessarily be something they love as much as whatever will contribute monetarily but still allow them freedom to pursue a serious relationship or see to the needs of their households. Even serious careers often get put on hold indefinitely during the childrearing years.

In many cases, the early interests we pursue may only be stop-gap efforts on our journey to find identity and fulfillment aside from being someone's daughter, wife, or mother. Most often, it's not until we begin to feel more secure in our situations that we finally feel free, financially and otherwise, to explore our own original interests.

No wonder it's not uncommon that when the guys have given out, we gals are often just getting started. You might say that when it comes to careers and ongoing interests, women are like cats—they have more than one life.

As stated before, many of us are good at a wide variety of things. Still it takes a while to discover our true identity, passion, and purpose. Like the items in the ironing basket that have gone out of style, many interests are merely passing fads or fancies, things we enjoyed doing for a while or thought we might be good at, only to discover they're not necessarily where our talents or energies are put to best use. Perhaps these are things we observed others doing and sought to emulate, only to discover that either we were ill-suited for them or, like the Nehru jackets and psychedelic prints of the '70s, the appeal was short-lived. Whatever the case, with no primary passion to sustain us, we soon lose interest.

Then there are the gifts or talents that were valuable for a certain season, but now, entering a different phase of life, neither the need for that gift nor the desire to do it still exists.

In the early years of our ministry, my interest was primarily in working with children. It was something I enjoyed, especially since my own children were young, and I possessed the energy, creativity, and organizational skills to do successfully. Now my children are grown, and we've taken on a higher level of ministry responsibilities. Though I still love children, even if the opportunity presented itself, I would no longer have the desire, patience, or energy to work with them on a full-time basis. This illustrates the ironing basket items that over the years we quite simply outgrow.

Whatever the case, through process of elimination, we eventually come to recognize our strengths, weaknesses, and limitations. No longer do we want to try and do it all. Been there, done that, got the too-large T-shirt. Now we're looking for something custom-made in our size and shape. We've come to the bottom of the basket, so to speak.

And surprise! There they are. A few select items bearing the wrinkles of neglect, but, to our great delight, they still fit and have never gone out of style. These are the unfulfilled hopes and dreams that may now be worth shaking out and pressing to our hearts.

The question is "What do we do with them?" The first order of business is to determine whether something is still interfering with our putting them on and wearing them. Is it circumstances, people, money, all of the above?

In the case of circumstances, we may discover that it's still not immediately possible or wise for us to simply drop everything and take off on some deluded detour. All of us have made certain choices in life. Whether we have chosen to be wives, mothers, career persons, or pursue full-time ministry, these are examples of things that carry not only certain responsibilities but also serious spiritual commitments. One choice often leads to another. Except in extreme cases, we have a God-given obligation to buck up and be patient, staying put until the situation smoothes out or the time comes that we know God has released us from that particular set of responsibilities. Still, there may be steps we can begin to take toward making our goals a reality, even if it means just beginning to formulate a practical plan.

As for the people in our lives, they're part of the plan for our lives. They provide us with invaluable experiences, causing us to grow and change. Often they're our best supporters and encouragers. If they seem to be preventing us from pursuing our dreams, perhaps it's because, fearing it might sound shallow or silly, we've never taken the time to share our deepest heart's desires with them. Even those who love us the most don't always know us the best, and they're not mind readers. Maybe it's time to get them into the basket.

Finding the resources needed to make our plans materialize, monetarily or otherwise, can undoubtedly be one big wrinkle. Yet doesn't Ps. 50:10 tell us that the cattle on a thousand hills belong to God? Then certainly He can make provision for the wishes we're wool-gathering in our own small pastures.

Let me just say here that when my opportunity for publication finally came, it was my husband and family who were among my best encouragers and supporters. As well, project by project, any finances needed somehow always presented themselves. I can also attest that God will provide the encouragement we need to keep us going.

It was only after a couple of minor publishing successes that I finally dared to begin believing that God was opening a new door of ministry for me in the area of my much-loved writing. Even with no future publishing prospects, I decided to take a step of faith. *What does a real writer need?* I asked myself. *Of course—a computer.* So I started saving my income from sporadic speaking engagements. In the meantime, I began attending some local writers' conferences to hone my skills. This all took a while, and at times I questioned the wisdom of the financial output I was making. Just as I was beginning to think my dream might have been a result of the cold pizza I ate the night before, something wonderful happened.

One evening my husband and I attended a large meeting of ministers in our area. Unexpectedly, the wife of the host pastor called us to the platform and presented us with a bag containing several small gifts. Imagine my amazed delight when one of the things I pulled from my gift bag was a computer mouse pad decorated with a lovely picture by an artist I admired. The thing that brought sudden tears of joy to my eyes, however, was a Charles Kingsley quotation printed across the top: "Have thy tools ready. God will give thee work." That dear lady had no way of knowing that she, herself, had been a tool in God's hands that night.

It should go without saying that the best way to be assured of success in our endeavors is to be sure the plans we're pursuing are committed to bringing God glory. "Delight yourself in the LORD," Ps. 37:4 instructs us, "and he will give you the desires of your heart." More accurately, I believe, as we commit our way to Him and seek His direction, He'll bring our desires in line with His. In that respect, we never have to worry about doing the wrong thing. Not for long, anyway. If we're truly seeking Him, God will open or close the doors.

For those who truly see themselves in a place of having little real control—trapped perhaps in a set of circumstances that were not of their choosing, or feeling that while God seems to open doors of opportunity for others, they're being passed by—let me offer this advice. Though in some cases we have little control over our immediate circumstances, Scripture makes it clear that we always have control over our attitude toward them. Otherwise how would the apostle Paul, sitting in a Roman prison with an uncertain future, have been able to write to the Philippian church in Phil. 4:11, "I have learned to be content whatever the circumstances"?

Does lack of control in this area make you feel angry, frustrated, or bitter? Even depressed? Don't expend the negative energy. Instead, put that energy into taking positive steps toward improving yourself and preparing for whatever it is you really feel God directing you to do.

For some it may be a matter of simply deciding how to better balance their responsibilities in order to find the time. Much of this depends on how strongly we feel about doing it. If it's something we're passionate about, we'll be willing to make some drastic changes, maybe even some serious sacrifices, to see it happen. This might mean going back to school or beginning to accumulate the tools needed to fulfill our true calling. Undoubtedly, just by taking some intentional steps in a positive direction, our outlook on the less-than-perfect set of circumstances will be improved.

As you look a little closer at your circumstances, ask yourself this question: Are the obstacles I see real or imagined? You see, it's not uncommon that the things we believe are keeping us from pursuing our passion are sometimes just—gasp!—*excuses*. Why? Because faced with the reality of a long-awaited dream, we may discover we're harboring some unconscious fear of failure or the unknown. Maybe this has even caused us to subconsciously sabotage or postpone our pursuit. In some cases we know the Lord has been telling us repeatedly that the time is right, but we keep procrastinating, perhaps dreading, the preparation or sacrifice we know it may require. Tom Peters said, "Unless you walk out into the unknown, the odds of making a profound difference in your life are pretty low."

In reality, most fear is based on not having enough information. We can build confidence by learning more about whatever it is we believe God is leading us to do and working to develop our abilities. "Obstacles," from automaker Henry Ford's perspective, "are those frightful things you see when you take your eyes off your goal."

Some things, however, we can't possibly know—that's where faith comes in. There's no point in worrying over the big picture when God is only asking us to focus the camera. The four energy-savers discussed in a previous chapter and found in Ps. 37:4-8 can apply here too. Commit your way to the Lord, seeking Him for direction and wisdom. Trust in Him for opportunity and provision. Keep hoping, and start planning, taking the needed steps to prepare yourself. Then be patient—it will be worth the wait.

The things we don't always have to wait for, of course, are the perfect conditions. My dear friend Elisabeth Sherwood, a pastor's wife from Chelmsford, England, refers to this as "chasing spiritual rainbows." "It's a thought that came to me once while praying about my deep desire to really serve the Lord at some future time," she states. "It suddenly occurred to me that if I think my significant spiritual life will happen only when circumstances are perfect or when some particular event happens, I will miss the present God moments in my life. It's like the man who sees a rainbow and runs for the pot of gold. I can spend my life frantically hoping I haven't missed my pot of gold, or I can see the rainbow and embrace the promise."

The writer of Proverbs puts it this way: "Hope deferred makes the heart sick, but a longing fulfilled is a tree of life" (Prov. 13:12). Who wants to feel sick when he or she can feel satisfied? We need not always wait to pursue our dreams until we're finished with other responsibilities or feel that we're fully prepared. Quite often the learning comes with the doing.

Here's where some of us get hung up again in the comparison snare, thinking our gifts are not as good as others. Let me share this exceptional word picture by an unknown author: "Use the talents you possess, for the woods would be very silent if no birds sang except the very best." You, my ironing basket buddy, have something no one else can offer. Don't rob others of that blessing.

Once again, let me slip in a bit of laundry lingo. Don't let anyone, including yourself, break your bubble. Though it may take a few years of figuring things out, the good news is that it's never too late. We may think too much water has gone through the washer, that we've missed opportunities, or that we're too old to pursue what we consider some youthful fantasy, but if the shirt still fits, sister, wear it.

I know what some of you are thinking. *Where in the world do I start?* Right where you are. Here's another divinely inspired little ditty from a fellow named Carl Brand: "Though you cannot go back and make a new start, my friend, anyone can start from now and make a brand new end." Start by asking yourself this question: *Where would I like to be five years from now?* In other words, what do you want to be when you grow up? Make a plan, and begin to grow in your best and most effective gifts.

Maybe some of you haven't quite ironed out where your true gifts lie. Let me give you some things to think about. First of all, what were your favorite things to do as a child? According to every old report card my mother saved, mine was to talk. "Judi would be a better student," one teacher wrote, "if she didn't socialize so much." Wouldn't she be surprised to discover how much of my time now is spent speaking at retreats? I also had a vivid imagination as a child, something that every writer requires to be creative. Both are "gifts" that obviously began to develop early, though perhaps my teachers wouldn't have called them that.

Here are a few more questions for consideration. What do people compliment you on? What do you really enjoy doing, and how often are you able to do it? What are you passionate or compassionate about? In her book *The Path*, author Laurie Beth Jones writes, "Our passion becomes our power."[1]

Perhaps by thinking about these things, you'll see a recurring theme beginning to develop. If so, there's a good chance that one or more of these may be the very gift that God is dealing with you about developing. You may not know the long-term plan that God has for you, but according to Jer. 29:11, He does. "'I know the plans I have for you,' declares the LORD, 'plans to prosper you and not to harm you, plans to give you hope and a future.'"

Remember, too—our gifts are not all the same or given just for ourselves. They're for the purpose of complementing and building up the Body of Christ. "To each one of us grace has been given as Christ apportioned it," Paul wrote. "It was he who gave some to be apostles, some to be prophets, some to be evangelists, and some to be pastors and teachers, to prepare God's people for works of service, so that the body of Christ may be built up until we all reach unity in the faith and in the knowledge of the Son of God and become mature, attaining to the whole measure of the fullness of Christ" (Eph. 4:7; 11-13). We're all part of bringing balance to God's greater plan.

Still feel you have some sorting to do or a few wrinkles to iron out? My best advice is to keep digging through that pile of prospects, growing, as instructed in 2 Pet. 3:18, "in the grace and knowledge of our Lord and Savior Jesus Christ." In that way He who began a good work in you will carry it on to completion. Somewhere in the ironing basket the perfect outfit will eventually emerge.

WASH-AND-WEAR
STILL HAS
SOME WRINKLES

Let patience have its perfect work, that you may be perfect and complete.
—James 1:4, NKJV

Even as I've been in the process of writing this book using lessons from the laundry, I'm acutely aware that many readers represent a generation who takes their clothes to the cleaners. And ironing? Forget about it. Most fabrics now are wash-and-wear anyway. We can simply shake 'em out and put 'em on. So why bother? If the wrinkles don't all come out—well, there's nothing wrong with a few wrinkles, right?

I have to admit there are some things about this laid-back latitude that I admire. My children and grandchildren don't seem nearly as concerned about appearance as my generation was. Neither do they sweat a lot of the small stuff that their parents and grandparents saw as essential to being well-balanced. In many ways that freedom is refreshing. Everything now is about comfort and convenience. The older I get, the more I've come to appreciate that.

A lot of it boils down to personal preference and individual outlook. No doubt cutting corners here and there provides extra time for other more important, pressing matters. Still I've had occasion to observe the profound negative effect this has on the patience in certain younger family members. In a world where most things can now be nuked in a nanosecond, they don't understand the necessity of waiting for anything. Fast food has taken its toll, in more ways than one.

Here's a great anecdote from my friend and fellow speaker Judy Rachels. Seems on a recent visit to her married son's house, Judy was sitting with her little grandson, Luke, in the family room, watching television. Even as cartoon images flashed across the screen, Luke kept up a steady stream of childish chatter. Just then a loud "ding" sounded from the microwave oven in the adjacent kitchen. Midsentence, he hopped up and headed toward the table.

"Where ya goin', Luke?" Judy called.

"Didn't you hear the *ding*, Nana? That means dinner's ready." Like Pavlov's experimental pup, seems today's young pups respond to a whole different set of stimuli.

No doubt about it—we live in an instant society, one that, from wash-and-wear to microwave meals, makes taking the way of least effort appear not just appealing but apropos. From a material standpoint, that's OK. My concern is the effect our shortcut society already seems to be having on this same generation spiritually.

I can just hear my son now saying, "Mom, you worry too much!" In my own defense and after some consideration, I've come up with a standard response: "That's because *you* don't worry *enough!*"

Here's my concern. Much of what's now happening in our churches seems to be focused on what makes us feel good, on receiving maximum blessing with minimum effort. What if the Early Church had taken this same approach? Maybe some did, and that's what prompted Pastor James of the First Christian Church in Jerusalem to write.

"Consider it a sheer gift, friends," reads James 1:2-4, translated in *The Message*, "when tests and challenges come at you from all sides. You know that under pressure, your faith-life is forced into the open and shows its true colors. So don't try to get out of anything prematurely. Let it do its work so you become mature and well-developed, not deficient in any way." Seems what James is telling them—and us—is that not only will we not escape stressful situations, but we should even be embracing them. Furthermore, we can't cut corners spiritually without losing the growth and maturity that come through discovering the purpose and patience in the process.

In light of that, perhaps it's time we stopped for a moment and counted the cost of convenience when it comes to our spiritual lives. Could it be that by taking a lackadaisical approach to difficult circumstances, we're short-circuiting the faith-building process in our lives, perhaps even putting ourselves in a position of denial and potential bitterness? After all, how many times have we all heard the question "Why does God allow bad things to happen to good people?"—as if because we're Christians we should be exempt.

It's when we find ourselves under pressure that things come out that we never expected or knew we had in us. To repeat a portion of the above passage, that's when our "faith-life" comes out and we "[show our] true colors." As one of my good preacher pals Donnie Moore puts it, "Circumstances don't make us who we will be—they reveal who we already are." Sometimes what we discover about ourselves is good, other times not so good, but one thing is for sure—only then are we forced to take inventory of the ingredients in our own personal pantry, to see what we have to work with.

Sometimes we're amazed at the inner resources we possess, especially when we consider, as Donnie also says, that "God shows His confidence in us by the circumstances He sends our way." That can't help but either build our own confidence a bit—or make us wish He didn't trust us so much!

Undoubtedly, however, God will allow some circumstances to come our way so we will recognize our limitations. Why? It causes us not to get so cocky and forces us to relinquish the reins, conceding once more our great need of God. Only then, as we learn to depend on Him and see what He's able to do either in or *despite* us, does our faith begin to grow.

One thing is for sure. We all have a lot of stuff spinning around in our lives. Things can't just tumble on forever or lie there in a big lump in hopes that everything will turn out OK. Even wash-and-wear comes out wrinkled if we're not diligent to take the garments out of the dryer in a timely fashion.

How easy it is to get distracted and forget what's most important! We need to train ourselves to listen for the divine *ding*. This means paying more attention to even the smallest details of our daily lives. How often does God attempt to speak to us through some seemingly insignificant situation, but we're too busy to pay attention?

A few years ago, struggling through a new cycle of difficult circumstances with our children, I came to a place in which I wondered if God heard me at all. It seemed I had prayed every way I knew to pray, and nothing was changing for the better. At the time, we happened to be living temporarily in a small, rented duplex whose best feature was a back porch that overlooked a lovely pastoral valley. Early one morning I stepped outside to simply sit in the quiet, allowing that serene scene to soothe my troubled spirit. There in the silence God began to speak, impressing me to be patient a while longer but offering me His presence and His peace. In tearful gratitude, I grabbed some paper and penned the following prayer:

God, I am waiting in your silence. Help me to rest in it rather than become restless. Teach me without words—Spirit to spirit. Perhaps you are quiet so that I must press in to hear, learning to tune out the voices around me and find the frequency of your voice alone. Perhaps you are not silent at all. I am just not listening loudly enough.

Though we don't like to think of it, there may come a time in our lives when it seems we'll never get the wrinkles out of our wash-and-wear worlds. Things have tumbled around for so long that when we open the dryer, we discover nothing left worth drawing out. That's when God comes to remind us that He's still the Creator, the Master of making something out of nothing—that He who created the cosmos out of chaos is still in the business of working modern healing miracles.

This confirms my belief that there's still something to be said for starting from scratch.

I learned to cook from my mother, who rarely ever made anything from a mix. I can still see her in the kitchen, chopping, mixing, and slaving, as the old saying goes, over a hot stove. Her meals were truly labors of love. Many of them included fresh vegetables grown in my dad's summer garden. As a kid, I probably took a lot of what went into making those meals for granted, but years later, learning to replicate them for my own family, I came to truly appreciate what goes into the process.

I also learned that certain ingredients and specific instructions were required to make things turn out the right way. A few times over the years I've found myself short of an ingredient or two. What I discovered is that when we've been taught what works in a recipe and what doesn't, we can sometimes make substitutions and still produce a delectable dish.

As we submit ourselves to God's growth process in our lives, we learn never to take for granted what He pours into us. It's through this process that we gain the experience and wisdom to make wise future decisions. Only when the lessons are fully learned might He allow us to cut a corner or two.

Creating something original takes time. Aren't you glad that God sees each one of us as a unique creation, that He chooses ways of teaching us things that are individually suited to our needs and circumstances? I don't know about you, but I don't want to short-change that creative process.

As a writer, I've learned that anyone can put words onto a page, but "creating" means reaching into the deepest recesses of your soul to see what, if anything, you really have worth saying. "Out of the overflow of the heart," Jesus said in Matt. 12:34, "the mouth speaks." Just like money in the bank, something has to be deposited in us before we can make withdrawals. Spending time in God's Word and prayer, not taking shortcuts when it comes to waiting for answers and allowing Him time to work in our lives— these are the daily deposits we're making. These are the promises we can take to the bank.

Seems that every day you hear someone advertising a new-and-improved product. Kind of makes you wonder what was wrong with the old one, doesn't it?—or if they'll ever really get it right. It's quite clear that we can't depend on the world's technology to make life perfect. As long as we live, even the most futuristic fabrics are undoubtedly going to get a few wrinkles when the heat's on.

Take heart. Only God knows what we'll have to face in the future, yet every experience He allows in our lives is to prepare us for whatever comes next. That's why we must let patience have its perfect work, so that we can be perfected as well. Verse 24 of Jude reminds us that it's He alone who is able to keep us from falling and present us before His glorious presence without fault and with great joy.

Finally—a robe with no wrinkles. Won't that be heavenly?

FABRIC SOFTENERS

I thank my God every time I remember you.
—Phil. 1:3

What can possibly be better than a clean load of softly scented laundry that has just come out of the dryer? Something about the warmth and aroma begs us to bury ourselves in it. True confession: I've been known to do just that—especially if it's a cushy comforter, a warm woven blanket, or a plush pair of socks on a cold winter's day.

This is how I like to think of the wonderful women God has brought into my life over the years to soften and sweeten my load, not to mention conserve the color. Undoubtedly many have provided a blanket of warmth and comfort when the world around me seemed cold, unfair, and unforgiving. Haven't we all had them—friends, teachers, and relatives, someone who provided positive input and brought balance? Surely if we take the time, each of us can recall at least one mentor for every milestone.

Aside from my own mother, the first memory I have of one who exerted a profound influence in my life became the subject of an article I recently wrote for *Woman's Touch Magazine*.[1] Maybe it will serve as an example, even remind you of a special someone in your own life. Here's how it goes.

She wore her gray hair twisted into a bun at the base of her neck, just low enough to show under the stylish hats popular in the '50s. We never knew her age, just that she was really old—55, at least. But what did it matter? Every week she told us stories about Jesus, and on our birthdays, the entire class got invited to her house for a Sunday afternoon party complete with fried chicken and chocolate cake. Her love for the Lord and for us was so real. We knew her simply as Sister Jarvis, our fourth-grade Sunday school teacher and, for that year at least, our very best friend.

Make no mistake, though. Graduating from her class didn't mean Sister Jarvis stopped caring. Forever after she took a special interest in "her girls." No surprise, then, that a few years later near Christmas she poked a large envelope into my hand. She'd heard I was taking piano lessons and wanted me to have a coveted piece of her own sheet music—a seasonal selection entitled "Put Christ Back into Christmas." But not before she imparted just one more lesson. "Christmas is getting too commercial, Judi. Let's keep reminding folks of the real meaning."

Placing the music on my piano stand later that day, I recognized her bold script on the upper right corner: *Esther Pearl Jarvis.* It was the first time I knew she had three names.

Sister Jarvis taught Sunday school for many more years, then lived independently well into her nineties —long after I'd gone away to college and married my minister husband. Though I've had many wonderful mentors over the years, it's amazing how those early lessons have remained the simplest yet truest fundamentals of my life and ministry. Love the Lord. Love others. And keep reminding people what is most important. Just like Esther Pearl, they were truly "pearls" of wisdom.

Maybe you weren't fortunate to have been brought up in Sunday school or have a teacher like Sister Jarvis. Still, I'm sure there have been others who have had similar influence.

Somehow thinking of those who have contributed to our lives in such a way reminds me of what were once called "quilting bees." These were gatherings much like the scrapbooking parties that are so popular today, but instead of pictures and keepsakes, women from the church or community brought scraps of fabric. Then, stitch by stitch, they worked together toward the common goal of constructing a beautiful and colorful quilted blanket such as the ones often seen hanging in someone's house or an antique store.

What a bonding experience it must have been! Sometimes they didn't even know what the pattern would be until all the pieces came together. Often mistakes were made, and it was necessary to go back and rip out a few stitches. It took time to evaluate which pieces were worth using and which needed to be discarded, which would ultimately provide the correct colors to make the most beautiful pattern. Spiritually speaking, I see these same similarities in our lives as women.

Undoubtedly a lot of life-pieces got sorted out and pieced together over those quilting tables as well. These were times that provided fellowship and instruction, while still resulting in a service to those who benefited from the final product. To me, this is the model a mentoring relationship should take: searching, sharing, benefiting, and blessing all those involved.

Most often it was the older women who taught the younger. Ever stop to think that none of us would have any wisdom or knowledge if someone hadn't taken the time to teach us? Not a bad thing to remember when we're tempted to expect too much from others—or from ourselves, for that matter. Not only do none of us automatically know it all, but some of us are slow learners. We need all the support, encouragement, and influence we can get.

"A true friend," says William Arthur Ward, "knows your weaknesses but shows you your strengths; feels your fears but fortifies your faith; sees your anxieties but frees your spirit; recognizes your disabilities but emphasizes your possibilities." They also give you someone to call when you don't know where else to turn, something we all need when life gets a little overwhelming or the path takes an unexpected twist.

How well I remember!

By the time my children had begun to come along, we were once again living in Alaska but had settled in the larger city of Anchorage. This time my husband had taken a position at a fairly large church, which kept him very busy. Our three boys were all under the age of five and quite a handful. It didn't take long for me to see I needed more help than my husband alone could possibly give.

These were the years when, as a new mom and minister's wife, I would ordinarily have been calling my own mother each day for advice. Being that far away, though, made it difficult. In those days long-distance phone calls were expensive, letters took a long time, and e-mail was still science fiction. Thankfully, the Lord provided me with two marvelous mentors for that mothering and ministry milestone.

One was a church board member's wife whose children, with the exception of one, were pretty much raised, so she had much invaluable experience to share. She was also fun and feisty, possessing a quick wit. Admittedly I often called her just to have a good laugh and hear another adult voice. How many times did she take moments out of her own busy schedule just to listen? Bless her.

The other was our senior pastor's wife and one of the greatest ministry models I've ever had. She was an accomplished Bible teacher, pianist, and hostess extraordinaire. Undoubtedly, though, the greatest lesson I learned was watching as she held her head high through the deep and devastating waters of an unexpected marital infidelity. She taught me that ultimately our deepest faith can't be in even those we love and trust the most—it must be in the Lord alone.

By the time our boys were nearly grown, we had moved to California and inherited a whole different set of parental problems. Again the Lord provided me with a wonderful pair of pals, the kind you could call in the middle of the night—which I did a few times. Down that painful prodigal path, my dear friends Catherine and Jacque kept me on track with their objectivity, positive spiritual perspectives, and hope.

How wonderful it is to know that we're not on life's journey alone, that the Lord causes special people to cross our paths, those who will come right alongside and walk with us. These are those who, if not older, are at least wiser and can be more objective in the course of our current situation. They're not only willing to take the time to teach and encourage us spiritually but are committed to giving sound advice and setting a solid spiritual example.

"Two are better than one," quotes the preacher in Eccles. 4:9-12, "because they have a good return for their work: If one falls down, his friend can help him up. But pity the man who falls and has no one to help him up! Also, if two lie down together, they will keep warm. But how can one keep warm alone? Though one may be overpowered, two can defend themselves. A cord of three strands is not quickly broken."

At the same time, we need those who will bring us to accountability, challenge us to be better, and help us to stand firm. A new online author friend of mine, Betty Southard, whose book *The Mentor Quest*[1] is all about discovering the many mentoring resources that surround us, says, "I do believe it is helpful to have an accountability partner, someone who loves us enough to confront us when needed. I have had a personal prayer partner with whom I meet once a week to talk and pray for many years. I firmly believe I am the person I am today because of this discipline. While we are peers and don't mentor in the traditional way, our commitment to upholding each other, our families, and our ministries in prayer have certainly been part of a mentoring relationship."

Somehow these special "softeners" assist us in smoothing out the wrinkles without tweaking the true and unique texture of our lives. They love us as we are but also see God's potential in us. "The greatest glory to God," says Randy Raybrook, "results when each person is accepted in light of his own history, treated with a divine sense of time and timing, and loved with a sense of anticipation as to what he will become." It seems obvious that this requires someone who knows us well and has a personal interest in us, our families, and our future.

Recently I've been introduced to a new trend toward something called "life coaches" or "spiritual directors." These are either laypeople or those with some type of ministerial credential who have dedicated themselves to taking on the task of mentoring, usually with some sort of fee involved. I don't doubt there are circumstances when this is a good thing. Still, I would counsel some prayerful caution before entering into any type of contracted companionship of this nature. To my way of thinking, mentoring is a calling, not a career. I still believe God is the best matchmaker, pairing us with those whom He has chosen for a particular purpose and selected season of our lives.

So, you may be wondering, what if these fine folks don't just fall into our laps? How else does one go about finding such a friend and mentor? Betty has a suggestion. "My belief is that if we are willing to develop 'mentoring eyes'—that is, accept the responsibility to look for the mentors we need—God will provide just what we need when we need it. Mentors come in different forms, and we must look for them purposefully."

"We will find direction in Scripture," she continues,

"and mentors among our family, friends, pastors, and professionals, even leaders of the past and younger Christians who come to us for aid." She states that even coworkers and neighbors can sometimes mentor us in some special way. Because our areas of expertise differ, we may even find ourselves mentoring the same people who have mentored us.

This was certainly the case with my good buddy Jan Coleman. Jan and I met at a writers' critique group sponsored by a mutual friend. It took each of us about three meetings to recognize two things: the group was too diversified to meet our personal needs, but writing-wise, we were on the same wavelength. While I knew Jan had the experience to help me develop my writing skills, the Lord knew we had a lot more in common than that. One follow-up phone call led to a five-year-and-counting friendship that finds us encouraging each other on a weekly basis not only in our writing but also in relationships with our prodigal children and a plethora of other predicaments.

Take a recent phone call for instance. I could tell by the way Jan answered the phone that she wasn't her perky self. Since it was right before Christmas, I could guess the reason. Jack Frost was nipping at her nose and giving her a mild case of the blues because her oldest daughter was mad at her. Though I had initially called to talk writing, instead I said, "Grab a cup of tea, and let's talk."

I knew Jan didn't need solutions, just a warm and familiar "I know." And I do. Many times has it been me on the receiving end of the telephone line. How great it was about

20 minutes later to hear Jan say, "I feel so much better already." That's what being a friend and mentor is all about.

Betty sums it up nicely: "Nothing happens to us that has not already happened to someone before us. If we're willing to look for the answers, God will supply the mentors we need for each situation." So true.

Let's go back for a moment to the above scripture from Eccles. 4 that speaks of a cord of *three* strands not being easily broken. The real assurance we have of success in any mentoring relationship is to include God as the third person in the partnership. Jesus speaks of the Holy Spirit as being our Counselor and Comforter. "I will ask the Father," He tells the disciples in John 14:16-17, "and he will give you another Counselor to be with you forever—the Spirit of truth." In the original Greek, the word for "counselor" is *paraclete*—one who one comes alongside, who, even when others forget or forsake us, is always there.

Whether the Lord comforts us himself or uses a special selected someone, we have an obligation to pass on the blessing. 2 Cor. 1:3-4 states, "Praise be to the God and Father of our Lord Jesus Christ, the Father of compassion and the God of all comfort, who comforts us in all our troubles, so that we can comfort those in any trouble with the comforts we ourselves have received from God." You see, it really isn't all about us.

I'm a firm believer that God brings certain people and circumstances into our lives to produce an ultimate thing of beauty. Some have short-term influence, some long-term, but all leave a bit of themselves with us. As someone once said, "We're no different five years from now than the people we've met and books we've read."

This reminds me of something I've recently realized. Some of our best mentors are people we've never even met. *How can that be?* you're wondering. They are those whose writing or speaking has been used by God to make real differences in our lives.

Betty speaks to us again from the pages of her own experience: "Since we need more help than we can get from personal relationships alone, we can also learn to see the mentoring potential in sermons, conferences, radio and television ministries, and books (including the Bible) that help us benefit from the wisdom of fellow believers from long ago and far away. The possibilities are exciting."

This is something I can attest to firsthand. When I was 12 years old, someone gave me the book *Through Gates of Splendor*, written by Elisabeth Elliot. It is the firsthand account of the ministry and martyrdom of her husband, Jim Elliot, and four other missionaries who went to take the gospel to a then-unreached tribe of South American Indians, the Aucas. Needless to say, the story gripped my heart. Even more arresting was how God gave Elisabeth the courage to take her three-year-old daughter back into the jungles to live with the very tribe who had killed her husband, eventually reaching them all for Christ. That book sealed my own lifelong commitment to ministry and missions.

Imagine my excitement and awe when, only a few

years ago, I had the privilege of meeting Elisabeth Elliot, now well into her 70s, at a conference. I was finally able to tell her how she, along with others such as Ruth Bell Graham, Amy Carmichael, even secular writers such as Erma Bombeck, has been one of my lifelong mentors through her writings. I'm sure I'm not alone.

On the same subject, here's one more mentoring message from Betty: "Those who are so busy that they don't have time to find a mentor should remember that their bookshelves are probably full of them. I often ask the Lord to guide me to just the right book on my shelf to help me find the answers I need to a particular problem. He faithfully propels me to pull out exactly what I need for each situation."

Book on, Betty.

I wouldn't be much of a mentor myself if I didn't address the subject of why our lives sometimes come out a bit on the scratchy side when it comes to picking positive relationships. Again it often comes down to making a deliberate choice of the people with whom we surround ourselves. Another helpful exercise from my counselor cohort Robin may assist us with bringing this into balance.

First, we write down the names of everyone we have some sort of ongoing relationship with for, say, the past two years. Circle in green those who are life-giving, joy-giving, and who after spending time with, make us feel energized and more alive. These are people we walk away from smiling. Now circle in red those we walk away from feeling tired, depressed, or drained, perhaps even frustrated and angry. If there are those who neither give energy nor take it away, circle them in yellow. These are the "flat-liners," those who have no effect on us either positive or negative.

After doing this, make three columns titled "green," "red," and "yellow," and place the names under the appropriate categories. "Sometimes," says Robin, "just the graphic realization of how few green people we hang out with and how many red people we do is shocking enough."

The purpose of the exercise is obvious. We all are affected to one degree or another by the people who surround us and who we surround ourselves with. Though we can't completely avoid coming in contact with an agitator every now and then, we need to consciously start saying no to spending a lot of time with people who rub us the wrong way, actively making time for those who soothe and smooth.

Robin tells of one client who came for counsel over depression. Come to discover, she spent 90-percent of her time with "red" people, that is, those who were depressed, complainers, whiners, negative, even ill. Like all of us, this woman desperately needed some fabric softeners—those who are spiritually and emotionally healthy, helping to balance and beautify the loads in our lives.

Perhaps you don't feel as though you have much to contribute when it comes to mentoring someone else. It might help to remember that everyone is in the process of becoming. None of us have arrived. Even as we're learning, we have something we can pour into the lives of others.

Sometimes we get only one chance.

As a speaker, I'm acutely aware that I often get only one opportunity to say something that may make a difference in someone's life. That can be especially true for people we meet in passing, which is why we should never miss an opening into which we might drop a nugget of encouragement. Want some real fabric softening fun? Learn to commit random acts of kindness, and watch the reaction.

Remember Eph. 4:7? "To each one of us grace has been given as Christ apportioned it." The key word in that scripture is "grace." God through Christ gives us the grace as we're piecing our own lives together to benefit from and contribute to the pattern in others. After all, you don't bring a completed scrapbook to a scrapbooking party—just the parts you're working to put in order.

That's the beauty of the Body of Christ—everyone has something to contribute to the whole. Like the pieces of a puzzle, we'll never see the big picture without the contributions others make to our lives and vice versa. If, as we learned in school, the whole is the sum of its parts, how much more is the whole person the sum of the people and experiences that have influenced him or her.

Doesn't it just make you feel warm and fuzzy all over?

CELEBRATING THE STYLES AND SEASONS

There is a time for everything, and a season for every activity under heaven
—Eccles. 3:1

Imagine with me for a moment all the styles of washers, types of fabrics, and loads of laundry that women have had, worn, and done over the last 100 years. No doubt about it, gals—we've collectively waded through a lot of wash. Fortunately there have been some major improvements in every area. Why is it, then, that though our workloads and wardrobes have never been easier to maintain, our lifestyle seems harder than ever to balance? I believe it's because we don't take enough time to sit back and celebrate the many styles and seasons that comprise the laundry of our lives.

Here are a couple of things I've learned about styles and seasons. First, what spins around once usually spins around again, just in some different form or fabric. Second, though some things last only for a season, every season brings changes and challenges that prepare us for the next. As both repeat themselves, the hope is that we learn enough from each not to repeat the same mistakes twice. Of course there's always the possibility, as someone once said, that if we don't learn the lesson the first time, God will keep repeating it until we get it right. Maybe that's not so bad.

Some things, life-wise and otherwise, are simply more obvious than others. Take that unfortunate plaid polyester leisure suit phase from the '70s, for instance. Who would want to repeat a mistake like that? Likewise, common sense and experience caution us to stay away from certain things that we might have earlier in life thought little of tossing into the washtub.

Other things in our lives are mandated by maturity. While I find a few of today's youthful styles appealing, there's no way at my age and weight I would be caught dead in some of them. Likewise, the older I get, the more I realize there are some things God knows I just don't wear well spiritually—like bitterness. My good friend Joan Butler has a simple saying I love. Anytime she hears someone whining over some unfair situation in life, she's quick to quip, "Girlfriend, bitterness does not become you." So true.

It's the things that aren't as obvious we continually have to sort out. This may require us to spin and agitate through a series of cycles. The hope, of course, is that eventually the solutions to these situations will all come out in the wash.

Either way, King Solomon and I, with only a few centuries in between, have come to the same conclusion. Life is an ongoing cycle full of beginnings and endings. The problem is that sometimes it feels more as if we're going in circles than cycles. What, asked Solomon, is the point? Don't we all wonder at times? Here's what *we* decided. God has a season and time for every purpose. Our best hope is to keep trusting His timing. Meanwhile, attempt to live every day to its fullest.

The benefit of surviving a few seasons is to realize finally that we must not get so busy living life that we forget to look at life. Perhaps the most divine discovery, though, is that by serving and obeying God, we truly can live happily ever after—maybe just not here. 1 John 2:17 reminds us that "The world and its desires pass away, but the man [or woman] who does the will of God lives forever." The sooner we learn that lesson, the less a lot of other things will matter.

We can find joy and fulfillment in the simplest everyday things while learning important lessons from them. How? By taking time to find the hope and humor in nature, human and otherwise, until we inevitably discover the wisdom rooted in its rhythmic and unfailing cycle of seasons. Solomon wrote a book about that, too. What a coincidence!

Here's how he summed it up: "What has been will be again, what has been done will be done again; there is nothing new under the sun" (Eccles. 1:9). Even so, according to the same source, "there is a time for everything, and a season for every activity under heaven" (Eccles. 3:1). In chapter one we talked about the deceptive danger of being told we can do it all. Yet according to Solomon, given enough time, seems we could actually come close—just not all at once.

One major misconception many of us have is that once we mature, we'll have a better handle on keeping our lives in balance, thus more time to relax and enjoy life. I wish someone would tell me at what magical age that happens. Seems the older I get, the more responsibilities I have and the more realistically I'm forced to look at life. I hate it when that happens. The way I see it, you live here on earth only once. I wholeheartedly agree with architect Frank Lloyd Wright, who said, "The trick is to grow up without getting old."

I'm living proof that growing up doesn't necessarily mean getting old, or vice versa. Sometimes I embarrass my kids and grandkids with my silly, spontaneous actions. Take for instance a jacket I recently ordered from a catalog, light brown suede with long fringe hanging from the sleeves and yoke—sort of like something the historic sharpshooter Annie Oakley might have worn. I had wanted one of those jackets ever since I was nine years old. Surprisingly, when I mentioned it to my much-more-conservative husband, he said "Go for it." Maybe he's lightening up a little in his old age too. So I did. It's hard to explain how putting on that jacket makes me feel—frivolous, lighthearted, and, yes, years younger.

The reality is that growing up does sometimes dictate the demise of a number of youthful fantasies, but it doesn't have to mean the death of your dreams. There's a difference. And if you're able to reclaim a fun fantasy or two along the way, that's what I would call one of the "fringe" benefits.

Seriously, if we're intentional in the way we live, it may actually mean having the time and money to do things we always wanted to do when we were younger. On the other hand, we discover that some things that once mattered so much now no longer carry the same significance.

One of the critical shifts we must make, according to lifecycle experts, is from doing things right to doing the right things. We can do that only by knowing who God is and what He expects of us. In his book *Half Time: Changing Your Game Plan from Success to Significance*, author Bob Buford says this: "Halftime is the perfect opportunity to shift from trying to understand God to learning to know Him. It is the time to humbly accept the fact that you may never fully understand Him, but that you need to accept, on faith, that you are known and loved by him."[3] That knowledge alone can make all the difference, freeing us, finally, to pursue life's most important paths and possibilities.

No doubt this requires us to make some periodic reassessments—not always a pleasant prospect, if the following entry from my journal dated January 1, 1998, is any indication:

> The Braddys started the day with one of those discussions. Oh, come on—you know the kind. Thoughts and feelings have been building up for a while, and when the dam finally breaks, you are both surprised at what spills over. For a while you wonder how good the new year will be when it starts this way. Then the flood is over, the "water" is at a manageable level, and you begin to examine the foundation (not to mention your head) for cracks.

> Maybe some people in California [perhaps now I should add Louisiana] would not agree, but floods may not necessarily be all bad. True, they sweep away the stuff that we believe is essential to sustain life, the everyday stuff we cling to so dearly. Hopefully, however, what's left is the real inner Spirit on which we're able to rebuild our lives and nurture those we love.

> We humans just don't like taking the time to start over. But after all, isn't that what a new year is all about, whether it begins on January 1 or some random Thursday? It's a time of reflection, assessment, and the resulting resolution to, if not rebuild entirely, do some much-needed remodeling. How I thank God for another chance to do that!

> In our case, it came down to making sure we didn't lose "us" in the swift current of life changes. It has been two years of great challenge, but more than

that, it is the irrepressible feeling that of all the changes over all the years, this year is somehow pivotal. It most certainly has something to do with reaching that half-century mark; realizing that our parents, all but one, are gone and how much we miss their love and advice; our children are grown yet still need our love and advice (not to mention a few bucks here and there); and our grandchildren are arriving to bring joy and assurance that, regardless of our success or failure, something of us will live on.

Call it mid-life something-or-the-other, it arrived at our house on January 1, 1998. I hope no one will be too disappointed to learn that even district superintendents and their wives are not immune to the struggle of change.

Face it—some of us don't care much for change. We might even find ourselves wishing that every season were the same; at least then we would know what to expect. Perhaps in the beginning that's the way God intended it. After all, didn't His plan for humanity begin in a garden—a perfect place, scripture tells us, with ideal conditions? Then He created man and woman, and the fig leaves started falling. Guess we have no one to blame that one on but ourselves. Too bad. Seems that if humanity hadn't fallen, we would all be wearing bermudas year-round. That would certainly make my husband happy.

As for me, I enjoy the seasons. I like the fact that each is different, full of variety, wonder, and anticipation. My personal favorite is fall. Though some see autumn's brilliance only as the transient precursor to a season of bleakness, I believe if we would pause to reflect more closely, we would observe its tapestry of latent promise. Pick up a leaf. Examine its intricate edges, veins, and stems. God made each one unique and special. Under each tiny, scalloped acorn turret lies the potential for another mighty oak. Just like us. Maybe I'm more reflective than most, but I don't understand why it is we don't take more time to savor the seasons. Seems we're so anxious to get from one to the other that we miss the amazing value and wonder in each.

The same applies to the seasons of our lives. Certainly God takes us through many life cycles. There will be spring seasons, in which we sense that He's doing something new and fresh; summer seasons, in which the conditions are just right and growth takes place rapidly; autumn seasons, when we're desperately trying to hold on while everything around us is changing; and winter seasons, when we must wait in the cold silence and wonder if we'll ever again feel the sun's warmth and the stirrings of life. Yet God does nothing without purpose. Just like the physical seasons, no season of our lives is any less important than another in terms of preparing us for the next.

The best news is that just as God walked in the garden with Adam in the cool of the day, He walks with us through each and every cycle of lives. That alone is something to celebrate.

Maybe it all comes down to dressing for success. Despite the commercial touting cotton as "the fabric of our lives," we all know that different times of the year require us to wear different types of clothing—wool in the winter for warmth, linen and cotton to survive the summer's heat. When it comes to washing, these fabrics have to be handled very differently.

In the same sense, we can't expect to handle every season of our lives the same. Anyone can grow and thrive under ideal conditions. When those times come, we should enjoy and make the most of them. As things begin to heat up, however, it will be necessary to apply caution and keep a cool head. Any time of change will find us grasping for something that feels familiar. That's when we must fix our eyes on Him who is the same yesterday, today, and forever. When the winter winds come, chilling us to the core, we may be tempted to despair. It's then we must bundle up in our Bibles and be careful about exposing ourselves to questionable choices and discouraging voices. Never make a major decision, we've been told, when we're angry, confused, or depressed. Whatever the season, a steady diet of God's Word will always be our best source of nutrition, strengthening us to trust Him through any pruning process He deems necessary.

Sometimes the climate in our lives can become so out of balance that we suffer damage. In those cases, it inevitably takes some nurturing, sheltering, and patience to recover. Often we're tempted to try to move on as if nothing had happened, but it's crucial that we take whatever time is necessary to be healed and restored. This may mean calling for help from a trusted friend, pastor, or Christian counselor.

For those who are in the season of raising children, bless you. This is perhaps the hardest season of all. Jason Robards, playing the patriarch character in the movie *Parenthood*, lamented, "Once you have children, you have them forever, no matter how old they, or you, get." My husband says they never really leave home until they get their stuff out of your garage—in which case any of ours could come back at any time.

Undoubtedly this is the season when it's easy to lose patience and perspective. The story is told of a young mom who, after putting her children to bed, changed into old slacks and a droopy blouse, then proceeded to wash her hair. As she heard the children getting more and more rambunctious, her patience grew thin. At last she threw a towel around her head and stormed into their room, putting them back to bed with stern warnings. As she left the room, she heard her three-year-old say with a trembling voice, "Who *was* that woman?" I suppose the moral of that story is that if all else fails, disguise yourself as someone else. Maybe then they'll listen.

Here are a few thoughts that may help bring things back into perspective. Children truly are our gift to the world. In their lifetimes they'll see and experience things we never did. How important it is that we not rush this season, taking the time necessary to nurture and give them the guidance that will produce healthy human beings, ones who will contribute positively to the world they'll inherit!

I used to jokingly say that when I offered my children as a gift to the world, it wrapped them up and sent them back. That's OK, because they're my responsibility and I love them. Of all our worldly possessions, our families are the only things we can take to heaven with us. Despite a few rough patches in the road toward raising mine, I'm trying my best to do that.

Another thing—there are some lessons that can be learned only as a parent. In the chapter of my book *Prodigal in the Parsonage* titled "Those Whom God Hath Joined," I state the following: "There are no two earthly relationships that reveal to us as much about God as that of husband and wife or parent and child. Trust, intimacy, commitment, unconditional love, longsuffering—just to name a few. Only by experiencing this particular brand of joy and pain can we truly comprehend the heart of our Heavenly Father, a Father who continues to love and is willing to forgive no matter the times He is rejected and hurt."

So hang in there, Mom. Not only will you make it through the childrearing season—you'll soon look back and wonder how it went so quickly. As the guy on the Men's Wearhouse commercial says, "I guarantee it."

Especially during the time our children are small, it's easy for us to feel that life is not allowing us the time to fully develop or make the most of the gifts God has given us. Be patient. That season may just not have come around yet. On the other hand, if it's a matter of not making time to prepare yourself, remember that there's no season like the present to think about turning over a new leaf. Maybe you're wondering whether you'll ever have the time or, worse, that time will run out. In that case "mum" is the word you need to remember.

In my garden I have a large wooden planter filled with chrysanthemums. I planted them there because, frankly, I didn't know what else to do with them. From spring through summer they continued to grow, staying green but producing nothing more than leaves. I had even thought of pulling them up to make room for something else. Then one crisp October day I walked out to find that the entire tub had literally burst into a blazing kaleidoscope of bloom. Seems it's the later part of the year, when many of the other flowers have faded, that mums really show their colors. Maybe mum's *your* word.

In 1 Thess. 5:24 we're told, "The one who calls you is faithful and he will do it." Do what? Complete the work He started in our lives for the purpose of presenting us blameless before God's throne. You can't beat a deal like that. At just the right times and seasons, God will bring to bloom every seed He has planted in us. The important thing is that we get neither too far behind nor too far ahead of Him.

The seeds may have been planted in you long before you even knew it. My daughter-in-law, Deirdra, had a tough time of it growing up. Her parents divorced when she was just a baby. Then when she was four years old, her mother dropped her off at her dad's house and didn't come back into her life until Deirdra was almost grown. During those difficult years in between, her father had several rough relationships, causing her to contend with a couple of short-term, not-so-supportive stepmothers until he finally met a lovely lady named Linda.

By the time Deirdra met my son, it was no surprise that she was a bundle of insecurities and anxieties. Their rocky first few years together didn't do much to help. Eventually, however, she began to discover her own inner strength and unique gifts, recognizing that God had a wonderful purpose for her life. How thrilled I was when, a few years ago, she and my grandson went forward at the end of a church service and surrendered their lives to the Lord!

It was some time later when she told me that as a small child crying for her mother, she often cried out to God as well, asking Him to help her. At the time, she didn't fully realize who she was talking to, yet she somehow knew God was there. We've talked many times about the fact that, despite the difficulties of her past, it was no accident God brought her into our family. The Lord has given us such a special love and relationship. He's also given me the privilege of watching Deirdra blossom, despite a few thorns, into a beautiful woman, wife, and mother.

Earlier in the book, I quoted the passage in Jer. 29:11 that reads, "'I know the plans I have for you,' declares the Lord, 'plans to prosper you and not to harm you, plans to give you hope and a future.'" Sometimes, though, we stop reading too soon. "Then you will call upon me and come and pray to me, and I will listen to you. You will seek me and find me when you seek me with all your heart" (vv. 12-13). God hears us and keeps His hand on us through every season of our lives, sometimes even when we don't know it.

If we live through enough seasons, all of us will face some good and bad days, yet if we look closely, we'll see we have much to be thankful for. No doubt much of life is a process that requires patience. Don't give up hope. You may be just around the corner from a completely new season of productivity in your own life. Just as one season follows another, so do the opportunities God gives us. He's still the God of second chances.

The important thing is that, looking back or looking forward, we take time to celebrate every style and season in our lives. Doing so will help us truly bring the big and little loads of our lives into balance.

A FRESHLY LAUNDERED LEGACY

Our children and their children will get in on this as the word is passed along from parent to child. Babies not yet conceived will hear the good news —that God does what he says.
—Ps. 22:30-31, TM

The old quilt was so frayed and faded I was almost afraid to wash it. *What if it disintegrates in the dryer?* I worried. It had belonged first to my grandmother, then to my mother. For a few years it was forgotten, folded in an old trunk in the attic of my parents' home. That's where I found it when my brother and I went back to clean and sell the house after my mother became ill and had to be placed in a care home near us.

Guess after all it's been through, one more wash won't hurt, I reasoned as I tossed it in the machine.

As the washer whooshed and whirred, common sense caused me to question why I was even keeping the old quilt. It had certainly seen better days. How much use did it still have? Then heart overruled head as I began thinking of the many pieces and stitches that had gone into creating it, not to mention all the people it had warmed and comforted over the years. Even the stains were symbolic, a mottled reminder that sometimes life gets messy. That quilt, like the people who contributed to it, was part of my heritage. It served to remind me of those who had gone before me, something that seemed especially important now in light of my mother's fast-failing health.

Without a doubt, my mother was the single most significant human influence of my life. She was a model homemaker who cooked, sewed, and kept an immaculate home. Even though she periodically worked outside the home, she somehow still managed to participate in my many activities and interests. How many nights did we sit around our little kitchen table, I sharing some childishly insignificant slice of my life and she listening? No matter how her eyes drooped as the hour grew late, or how early she had to get up, she had a way of making me feel that what I had to say was infinitely more important than a good night's sleep.

This was especially amazing considering that my mother was 40 years old when I was born. Yet if she ever felt old, she certainly never acted it or looked it. She kept up with current fashions and taught me all the beauty secrets she knew. "You're as young as you feel" was the motto she modeled.

When it came to cleanliness, Mom had two theories: No one is so poor that he or she can't afford soap, and it didn't matter how old or tattered any garment was—it could still be washed, mended, and used for something. That pretty-much summed up her philosophy about people too. Nobody was a lost cause who couldn't be redeemed and made useful. Sometimes you had to scrub a bit to get past the tarnished exterior, but what came out in the wash was always worth the trouble.

Over the years, Mom applied her special brand of "detergent" to countless lives, especially her own children. I have no doubt that it was this outlook on life that made me determine during the difficult years of raising my own children that whoever God brought into our lives through whatever circumstances, I would do my best to love. That has paid off in ways I don't have space to explain.

If someone had asked my mom what "having it all" meant, it would have been basically three things: God, her church, and her family. Everything else took a lower priority. She actively loved and served the Lord, her local body of believers, and her children and grandchildren until the day her illness made it no longer possible. Even then, it didn't keep her from praying. Her godly example became my spiritual legacy—one I strive in the midst of today's stressful society to emulate for my own children and grandchildren.

"Family faces are magic mirrors," says Gail Buckley. "Looking at people who belong to us, we see the past, present, and future." This reminds us of the most important reason we have for taking a long look at our priorities and striving to bring balance into our lives: so that we, too, can leave a freshly laundered legacy for future generations. "A good [woman] leaves an inheritance for [her] children's children," instructs Prov. 13:22, "but a sinner's wealth is stored up for the righteous." Seems those on the Lord's side win either way.

Perhaps that's why two years ago, anticipating a two-week visit from four of my grandkids, I decided to start a new tradition. I spent days transforming our backyard into a summer camp complete with tent, cots, and sleeping bags. The barbeque became a campfire for cooking burgers, dogs, and s'mores. From build-a-bear to bowling, daily activities were painstakingly planned. I also bought fun Bible study books for the three oldest, which we did each morning along with our long-established routine of bedtime Bible stories and prayers at night. The hand-painted sign tacked on the gazebo said it all: CAMP GRAMMA. It was a place where memories were made not only for a lifetime but also eternity.

Prov. 14:26 promises, "He who fears the LORD has a secure fortress, and for his children [and their children] it will be a refuge." Obviously being a Christian parent or grandparent is much more than fun and games. It involves planting spiritual seeds, instilling self-confidence, and providing a safe place to camp out when the world gets scary. A fortress and refuge—that's Camp Gramma.

Whether or not you had the privilege of a biblical upbringing or a happy home life, you have the profound privilege and opportunity of providing one for your own family, perhaps even starting a freshly laundered new legacy. God has preserved you for a purpose, just as He did the children of Israel. Even as Moses was about to hand over His own inheritance to Joshua, He spoke these words in Deut. 4:20: "But as for you, the LORD took you and brought you out of the iron-smelting furnace, out of Egypt, to be the people of his inheritance, as you now are." Whatever our past may be, God has an amazing, positive plan and purpose for our futures.

None of us should underestimate the influence we can have individually and collectively. Yet how often do we find ourselves wondering, *What difference can one person possibly make?* "If you think you are too small to be effective," states a Samoan proverb, "you have never been in the dark with a mosquito." Keep buzzing, Baby.

So how does one go about leaving a freshly laundered spiritual legacy? I'm glad you asked.

First and foremost, we must know the Source of our own spiritual inheritance and strength. God is the provider of unimagined opportunities, and our enabler as well. "Now to him who is able to do immeasurably more than all we ask or imagine," Paul writes to the Ephesians, "according to his power that is at work within us, to him be glory in the church and in Christ Jesus throughout all generations, for ever and ever!" (Eph. 3:20). And together we all say, "Amen!"

Though at times we may question our own physical and spiritual stamina, we never have to worry about God's well going dry. According to Phil. 4:13, "I can do everything through him who gives me strength." Not only is that good for us to know—it's the best encouragement we can pass on to our children.

Next, we must know our personal sphere of influence and responsibility. Perhaps few of us will ever be world-shakers, but all of us can be world-shapers by becoming involved and exerting influence over the people God brings us directly into contact with on a regular basis, whether at home, at church, or in our communities.

Don't be surprised, though, if we find ourselves taking the heat for it at times. More and more it seems the motives and intentions of Christians are being questioned, misconstrued, and misunderstood by the world. Sometimes, frankly, we bring it on ourselves. Still, I see this not as a reason to withhold compassion but as an opportunity to model it all the more. "Thanks be to God," says 2 Cor. 2:14, "who always leads us in triumphal procession in Christ and through us spreads everywhere the fragrance of the knowledge of him." Sometimes it requires a pretty warm setting for that fragrance to be released.

One of the best legacies we can leave our children is pride in our Christian teachings. We are the Church of the living God, washed in the precious blood of Jesus—"a glorious church," one old hymn puts it, "without spot or wrinkle." Make no apology for it.

This brings me to one very practical way we can influence our families and prepare them for what the future holds. That is by making ourselves aware of current events and issues.

My husband is what I call a "newsaholic." He just can't seem to get enough, often listening to the same news from several different commentators. "Remember, Honey," I often tease him. "It's news only once."

For a long time I avoided reading or listening to much news because it upset or depressed me. The problem is, if we don't know what's going on, we can't discuss or deal with it intelligently. Simply sticking our heads in the sand is not going to make it all go away.

In a world where so much is misconstrued, particularly in the realm of religion, being informed is the best way of passing on accurate information to our children and others. More than that, it's an opportunity for providing a biblical perspective. With today's complex and confusing issues, it's critical that we know what we believe and make sure our children know, too. It's not going get any better—trust me. Better yet, trust the Lord.

For this reason alone, we need to touch and influence as many lives as we can while there's still time. What better reason, as mentioned in an earlier chapter, to get in the habit of committing acts of kindness, of doing everything with excellence and passion. Look for something to do every day that will touch someone else's life. I believe any time in any way we express love and compassion in the name of Jesus, we've made a difference in that person's life. Someone once said that people may never remember all the things you say, but they will never forget what you do. Surely putting these things into practice will release a freshly laundered fragrance that sweetens and beautifies the lives of others.

Maybe at times it feels as if all we do is encourage and support someone else, leaving little time for ourselves. It might help to think that the accomplishments of everyone whom our lives touch in some significant way are our own accomplishments as well, in some small way. A few years ago I wrote a poem that I believe expresses this point well:

> Our lives touched yours, and we could see
> A glimpse of how 'twas meant to be
> In God's own plan.
> As we, though mortal men,
> Become extensions of His hand.
> We touch, we feel, we reach to heal,
> We meet and too soon part,
> But richer far are we at heart
> Because our lives touched yours.

Perhaps you're reading this and feeling you're too old or worn to be of any significant influence. This brings me back to the torn-and-tattered quilt belonging to my grandmother, mentioned at the beginning of the chapter. I remember very little about my mother's mother, because she died when I was only seven. The image I have is of a frail, elderly woman, bedridden because of a broken hip that never mended properly; but that's not the greatest memory I have of her. I can still remember her sweet smile and pleasant disposition despite her physical pain and confining circumstances as I sat on her bed as a child, stringing buttons. I see how my mother was very much like her. If I have only one inherited legacy to leave, that's how I want to be remembered.

The reality is that with the opportunity for travel we enjoy now, we have more wide-spread influence than our mothers and grandmothers ever hoped to have. This struck me last year after my husband and I attended a conference in southern California and were sitting in the Orange County airport preparing to go in two different directions —he back home for weekend ministry and I on to Las Vegas to speak at a women's retreat. I remember thinking, *This is something my mother would have never even thought of doing.*

Fact is, though my dad worked for Boeing Aircraft for 20-plus years, neither he nor my mother ever got on an airplane until the day it became necessary to air ambulance her to California. I, on the other hand, have had the privilege of traveling the world, due in great part to my husband's current ministry position. Not only has this allowed me to make friends and influence people all over the world, but it's also caused me to see the world and my own circumstances in a much different way—a worldwide view I also hope to pass on to my children.

I wouldn't be a writer worth her ink and paper if I didn't mention that journaling, which I touched on earlier, is another wonderful way of leaving a legacy for our friends and families. When I speak at writing seminars, I always tell people that there are more important reasons to write besides being published. If we don't write down our feelings, family histories, and favorite stories, they'll be lost to future generations. Everyone has a story worth telling.

Remember, too, that we're not the only ones writing things down as part of our heritage. God is keeping a record of our spiritual heritage as well. As one precious pastor's wife who had an amazing impact on my life often said, "God keeps books." I believe 1 Pet. 1:3-4 backs up her statement: "Praise be to God and Father of our Lord Jesus Christ! In his great mercy he has given us new birth into a living hope through the resurrection of Jesus Christ from the dead and into an inheritance that can never perish, spoil or fade—kept in heaven for you."

It all comes down to this. The reason it's so important that we find a way of keeping life's big and little loads in balance is so we don't miss the important opportunities God gives us to affect and impact the lives of others. Even then, we may never really know the influence we've had until we get to heaven. That, dear sister, is when it will truly all come out in the wash.

NOTES

The Unbalanced Land

1. Deb Haggerty: <www.debhaggerty.com>; <www.positive hope.com>.

2. Joanna Weaver, *Having a Mary Heart in a Martha World* (Colorado Springs: Waterbrook Press, 2001), 46.

3. Jan Coleman, *The Woman Behind the Mask: Trading Your Facade for Authentic Life* (Grand Rapids: Kregel Publications, 2005), 21-22.

What Happened to the Other Sock?

1. Coleman, *The Woman Behind the Mask*, 129.

2. Marnell Jameson, "Bouncing Back," *Woman's Day*, October 8, 2002, 67-70.

Sorting Through the Stinky Stuff

1. Richard A. Swenson, M.D., from online article "Overload: Learning to Live with Limits," reprinted from *Christian Counseling Today*, Vol. 4, No. 3, with permission of the American Association of Christian Counselors, Inc.

2. Ibid.

The Ironing Basket

1. Laurie Beth Jones, *The Path: Creating Your Mission Statement for Work and for Life* (New York: Hyperion, May 1996), 49.

Fabric Softeners

1. Judi Braddy, "A Pearl of Wisdom," *Woman's Touch Magazine*, May-June 2005, 25.

2. Betty Southard, *The Mentor Quest* (Ann Arbor, Mich.: Vine Books, a division of Servant, 2002).

3. Bob Buford, *Half Time: Changing Your Game Plan from Success to Significance* (Grand Rapids: Zondervan Publishing House, 1994), 74.

4. Judi Braddy, *Prodigal in the Parsonage* (Kansas City: Beacon Hill Press of Kansas City, 2005), 98.

ALSO BY JUDI BRADDY

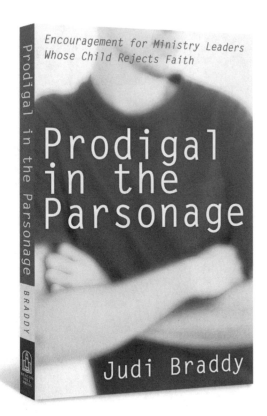

Prodigal in the Parsonage gives you, especially if you're in ministry, an insider's perspective and time-tested encouragement for struggling with trials that come when your child rejects faith.

Receive the insight and encouragement you need to endure the grief and anxiety of parenting a prodigal.

Prodigal in the Parsonage
Encouragement for Ministry Leaders Whose Child Rejects Faith
By Judi Braddy
ISBN-13: 978-0-8341-2206-2

BEACON HILL PRESS
OF KANSAS CITY

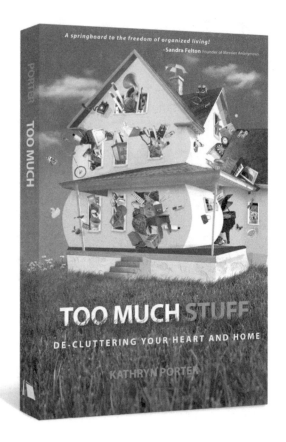

Where can you find the retreat you need?

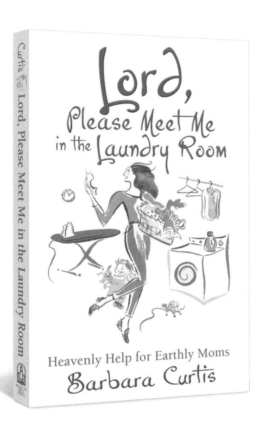

Lord, Please Meet Me in the Laundry Room brings ideas for spiritual retreats into the everyday life of busy moms. This book will unburden, enlighten, amuse, and encourage you in your hectic daily life.

Lord, Please Meet Me in the Laundry Room
By Barbara Curtis
ISBN-13: 978-0-8341-2097-6

BEACON HILL PRESS
OF KANSAS CITY